Introduction

Miniature quilts have won the hearts of quilters all over the world with their enchanting look and feel. They have many advantages over full-size projects. They are a delight to make, and you can easily find patterns for every skill level. They require little time and fabric, and are a great way to use scraps.

A miniature quilt makes a wonderful present for someone special, or you can use one or more to help decorate your home or workplace in a variety of ways. Many full-size blocks can be scaled down easily to a small but still manageable size to match, for example, a full-size quilt.

Even if you are not an experienced quilter, don't be afraid to try your hand at miniature quilt making. You are sure to have fun. However, be warned that making a miniature quilt is addictive—one is never enough!

Christine Carlson

Table of Contents

Cotton Nights,
page 23

Log Cabin Pineapple,
page 39

Nine-Patch Floral Garden,
page 46

House of White Birches, Berne, Indiana 46711   Clotilde.com

General Instructions

Getting Started

What Is a Miniature Quilt?

The expressions miniature quilts, small quilts and doll quilts are all synonymous. For the sake of simplicity, in many quilt books and magazines, small quilts are considered miniature, although there are some whose block size does not fit the miniature description.

According to many quilt-show guidelines, measurements for a miniature quilt cannot exceed 24" on any one side, with blocks no larger than 3" x 3". However, these measurements need further clarification.

Block size is only relevant when based on complexity. For example, a 3" Nine-Patch block will not appear miniature when placed next to another 3" block having many seams and block pieces. But a 1½" Nine-Patch block is considered miniature since each square in the block is only ½".

Quilt size is also only relevant when based on complexity. It is judged, for example, by the number of blocks—their difficulty, arrangement and size—and how the border is handled in relation to the quilt size.

A miniature quilt has many of the same elements as a full-size quilt, such as value, proportion, contrast and balance, and is, in many respects, a replica of a full-size quilt. However, one difference between the two is that the small intricacies of a miniature quilt encourage the viewer to come closer, while many full-size quilts are best viewed from a distance.

Color & Fabric

Scrap miniature quilts are exciting to make because the full impact of combining so many different fabrics will not be seen until all blocks are sewn together.

Needing special consideration, scrap miniature quilts differ from full-size scrap quilts because they require a planned color study due to their small size. Discrepant colors will stand out like a sore thumb. As a rule, handpick scrap fabrics in a controlled color combination.

If uncertain, think of putting a quilt together in terms of light, medium and dark fabric values so that you can still differentiate between the pieces. Then sort your scrap collection accordingly. To help achieve that scrappy look, search for prints in a variety of scales and designs, and from different eras.

Stick to a theme because this provides cohesion or a focus that will bind everything together. This is readily seen with the Kaleidoscope quilt (page 33) in which vivid colors coordinate with a border that is equally outstanding in color.

A coordinating color-and-fabric theme is found in the Fanciful Daisies quilt (page 43) in which antique fabrics all having the same look are used for both flowers and borders.

Assembly & Seams

During the block-assembly process, the measurements specified include the seam allowance. Seam pressing is indicated by little seams and directional arrows on the drawings for guess-free pressing. The quilt size given for each project includes the binding. All quilt pieces are identified with a letter to match assembly directions, including border pieces. The Supplies List specifies items needed for all aspects of sewing including thread and tools.

The use of a sewing machine and rotary-cutting equipment make for faster and more accurate piecing, and sewing with a ¼"-wide seam allowance allows for easy piecing.

Supplies List

If any special notions are needed for any quilt, they will be listed with each project. All projects require some basic sewing supplies and tools as follows:

1. Sewing machine with an accurate ¼"-wide seam allowance.

2. No. 65 or No. 70 machine needle.

3. A good-quality thread, such as Mettler Metrosene Polyester Plus thread, which may be found in any quilt shop.

4. 100 percent cotton fabric.

5. Small, sharp-tip fabric scissors.

6. Long, straight-head silk pins.

7. Magnetic pin holder—do not use with computerized sewing machine.

8. Fine-point seam ripper.

9. Stiletto—found at quilt shop.

10. Steam/dry iron and ironing board.

11. Light-body fabric spray sizing—found at grocery stores, sometimes called spray starch.

12. Small brass pins or white basting thread for layering.

13. A 1" x 12" C-Thru No. W25 ruler found at office-supply stores.

14. A ¼"-gridded plastic template product and marker.

15. Paper-cutting scissors.

Block Settings

Quilt blocks may be set several different ways—straight, side by side, on point or on the diagonal.

Side-by-side blocks can either be sewn together, or a sashing can be used to separate them. This is especially useful if there are a lot of seams to match. Adding sashing will automatically expand the quilt size as shown in Figures 1 and 2.

| Figure 1 | Figure 2 |

An example of a quilt with blocks set side by side is Spools Variation (page 50). An example of a quilt with blocks set side by side with sashing is Homecoming (page 56).

A little different example is the Churn Dash Delight (page 53). The pieced blocks in this quilt are set off using plaid squares to add a little interest to the background.

Setting blocks on the diagonal expands the quilt size and requires setting triangles. The blocks and triangles may be sewn together in diagonal rows or separated by sashing strips, which expands the quilt size even further as shown in Figures 3 and 4.

| Figure 3 | Figure 4 |

Diagonally set blocks also add visual interest. Look at the Dainty Baskets (page 59) whose points peak upward. Turned on their sides, these blocks would lack visual interest and appear quite ordinary.

The way a block is set can also change its appearance. When set side by side or straight, it has one look. When set on point, it takes on a completely different look as shown in Figure 5.

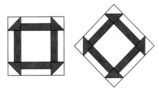

Figure 5

If undecided about how to set blocks, set up a viewing area that allows you to step back and look at each setting choice from a distance.

Floating Blocks

A quick-and-easy way to impart visual interest to diagonally set quilt blocks is to float them against the quilt background by using oversized setting triangles as shown in Figure 6. When the border is sewn on, there will be a measurable space between a block corner and border seam. This technique also easily expands the quilt size. Either a solid or a print fabric may be used.

 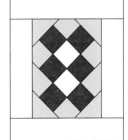

Figure 6

House of White Birches, Berne, Indiana 46711   Clotilde.com

Cut squares for setting triangles at least ¾" larger than required, even bigger if undecided—the bigger the triangle, the wider the space. The extra triangle fabric can always be trimmed down if the space is too wide.

The Dainty Baskets quilt on page 59 incorporates the use of floating blocks.

Tip

• *It is helpful to cut squares for corner triangles about ¼" larger than required. The extra fabric makes it easier to square the quilt-top corners before layering. Rounding up any odd-size measurements resulting in over-sized squares and triangles works in the same way.*

Choosing Fabric

Due to their small size, the most important and outstanding component of a successful miniature quilt is the effective use of color. The presence or lack of a winning coloration is the first thing that will be noticed instead of imperfect piecing or quilting stitches.

If stumped when choosing colors, overcome this by following a few general guidelines regarding value, contrast and proportion. Value and contrast go hand in hand—both are used to differentiate small quilt pieces and add visual interest.

Elements of Color

Value: Value refers to the significance or merit of a color. A fabric's value is determined by other surrounding fabrics. For example, place a medium-value color next to a light color, and the medium color will appear dark. Place this same color next to a dark color, and it will appear light (Photo 1).

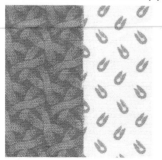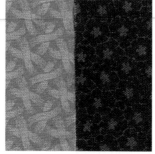

Photo 1. The blue/green fabric looks dark when placed with a light fabric but looks light in value next to the dark fabric.

Value is designated into categories of light, medium and dark as shown in Photo 2. There are degrees of value within each category, such as medium-light and medium-dark.

Photo 2. The first step in deciding value is to separate your fabric into light, medium and dark categories.

A quilt having all the same values, such as just light pastels, will not be as eye-catching as one in which the value is more dramatically defined. A poor use of color value can be seen in the Fans (page 30) quilt in which the setting triangles and squares are a medium value. The blocks would stand out more if a lighter value had been used for the setting pieces.

Contrast: To achieve contrast, use appropriate block background and/or quilt background fabric. The more contrast, the greater the differentiation. A good example of this is the Fanciful Daisies quilt (page 43) with a light background, which makes the blocks stand out.

Contrast is also achieved by varying or heightening the intensity of saturation of a color. For example, change from light to bright, such as pale yellow to golden yellow, or dark to deep, such as dark blue to midnight blue. This is especially applicable when working with only a few colors.

The decision about how much color to use should be based on the proportion or balance to the quilt plan and surrounding colors. For example, no one color should overwhelm others in piece size or intensity. A good example of this is the Homecoming quilt (page 56) in which the use of solid white does not overpower the total quilt plan, and in fact, picks up the white in the prints. The Log Cabin Pineapple quilt (page 39) is another good example, showing distinct colors that are not overwhelming.

Effective Use of Color

To use color effectively, work with a specific color family or scheme to enhance a quilt's theme, such as all Easter pastels, subdued earth tones or glowing, hot prints as shown in Photos 3–5.

Photo 3. Color schemes, such as these pastel prints, combine to give a spring look.

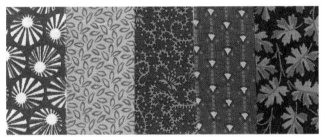

Photo 4. The earth tones in this collection range in value from light to dark.

Photo 5. The glowing, hot prints in this collection share geometric qualities.

Use color to convey a certain feeling or mood. Red, white and blue colors convey a patriotic message, dark colors convey a masculine or somber mood. Integrate a color recipe, such as country colors of cranberry, tan, navy blue and dark green. Look for the smallest pieces in a quilt plan and make them the most outstanding. Using all subdued solids brings to mind Amish-style quilts.

Draw on red, yellow and black colors to create movement as they cause the eye to move over a quilt to find its match.

Colors also impart temperature to a quilt. Pale green is soothing and tranquil, while a brilliant red appears hot and unsettling. If feeling lost, refer to a color wheel and choose colors in an uncomplicated format.

If uncertain of color placement, draw a block or quilt design on graph paper. Place lightweight tracing paper over it and start filling in spaces with coloring pens or crayons. When finished with one color family, replace the tracing paper and color again with a different color combination.

Hang up the various colorings, stand back and choose the most engaging and eye-appealing drawing on which to base your quilt.

Working With Fabric

Scale: Select prints in a variety of scale, from small to medium-small to keep them in proportion to the small scale of miniature quiltmaking (Photos 6 and 7). A medium-size print is useful for border or backing as shown in Photo 8 (page 6). A medium-large print may also be used for borders and backing if many of the print elements are small in scale as shown in Photo 9 (page 6).

Photo 6. Small-scale prints are perfect for miniatures.

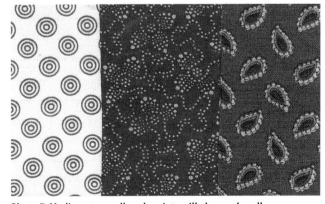

Photo 7. Medium- to small-scale prints will also work well in miniatures.

House of White Birches, Berne, Indiana 46711   Clotilde.com

Photo 8. Medium-size prints, such as those shown, may work in miniatures for borders, or for setting squares and triangles, but not in tiny pieces required in blocks.

Photo 9. Some medium- to large-scale prints will work for borders on a miniature quilt.

Texture: Add visual texture by incorporating a good variety and range of prints. This includes checks, plaids, stripes, florals, polka dots, calicos, pin dots, paisleys and geometrics as shown in Photo 10.

Photo 10. Use a variety of fabrics to create texture.

Movement: Create movement by using fabrics that accentuate direction such as directional prints, plaids, stripes or whirly prints. These add excitement to a miniature quilt.

Batiks: Working with batiks will give a more contemporary feel to your miniature quilt. The crispness of batiks and their dense thread count

will make for precise piecing in your mini. Batiks are available in a full suite of colors, in both tone-on-tone and multicolored variations.

Borders: Boldly patterned directional prints are excellent fabric choices for borders. However, remember that you are creating a miniature quilt and keep the scale of the print small (Photos 11 and 12).

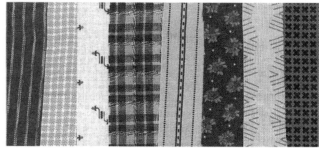

Photo 11. Directional fabrics add movement to a quilt and are perfect choices for borders.

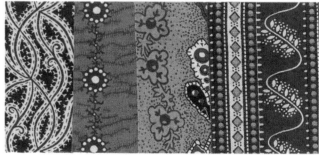

Photo 12. Movement is created by using boldly patterned border prints.

Centerpiece Print: Start fabric choices with a centerpiece print having no more than three colors (Photo 13). Use this fabric as a coordinating tool for remaining fabric choices. A fabric with an even or allover design (Photo 14) is preferable to one containing scattered designs as shown in Photo 15.

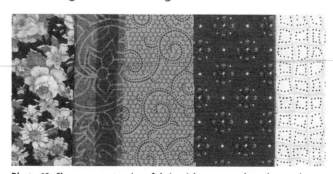

Photo 13. Choose a centerpiece fabric with no more than three colors. In this sample the centerpiece fabric is on the far left. Then choose fabrics to coordinate with the centerpiece fabric.

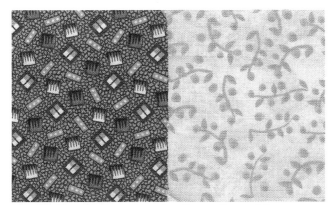

Photo 14. These fabrics are examples of even, allover prints.

Photo 15. These fabrics are examples of widely scattered prints.

Choosing Setting Fabrics: Use care when choosing fabrics for setting blocks and triangles. This fabric should complement, not compete with, the pieced or appliquéd blocks. Avoid a small, dense print as it can appear as a blur or a solid when viewed from a distance (Photo 16).

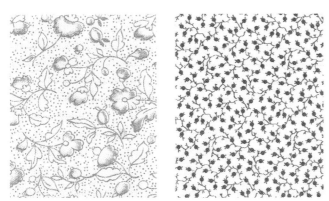

Photo 16. These prints do not make good setting blocks.

Using Solids: When a quilt is made with just solid fabrics, it is important to integrate colors that fit into a color category, such as all subdued country colors, all pastels or all intense colors. Use the brightest, lightest or darkest colors for small block pieces to make them stand out (Photos 17 and 18).

Photo 17. Subdued country-color solids in a range of darks and lights provide contrast.

Photo 18. Bright, hand-dyed solids make a cheery statement.

Hand-dyed solids add distinctive color and intensity when used in any quilt. Quilt shops also often carry a line of hand-dyed fabrics; avoid any of these fabrics that have a washed-out or dull look.

Auditioning the Fabric: If stumped when making fabric choices, try auditioning the fabric. Cut out a small geometric shape, such as a triangle or square, from a white sheet of paper to make a window; then place the window over the fabric to isolate the print. Start with a border print and work toward the center of the quilt for fabric and color coordination. Set up an audition area where fabric can be seen from a squinting distance.

Remember that the fabric choice is the first thing that will be noticed on a quilt. If it does not pass this first test, the viewer won't bother to take a closer look. Although there are no hard-and-fast rules, and a quilter may choose any color combination and any fabric she likes, it may or may not work to make a successful quilt.

House of White Birches, Berne, Indiana 46711   Clotilde.com

Construction Techniques

Miniature quilts require a few different construction techniques than those used on projects with larger pieces. This section will help you adapt your sewing skills for working the smaller pieces.

Your Sewing Machine

Many quilters who make miniature quilts like to hand-stitch their projects. Others enjoy using a sewing machine, and quick-cutting and quick-piecing methods. Some adjustments should be made for sewing on tiny pieces. The following methods/techniques work best when working with the tiny units needed to complete a miniature quilt.

Some miniature-quilt–making enthusiasts prefer to use a vintage Singer Featherweight sewing machine. This machine is known for producing fine, even stitches. Plus, the two feed dogs are closer together, and the presser foot is smaller than those on larger machines. This aids in sewing small pieces. The straight-stitch throat plate has a small round hole rather than an oval one, which prevents the machine from chewing up the ends of pieces when starting to stitch.

If using a standard-size sewing machine, look for one with a round hole in the throat plate and a clear plastic presser foot. Single-hole throat plates can be purchased separately for most domestic sewing machines.

Tips

• *Stay with the same sewing machine for the entire project. Switching machines mid project can cause a slight difference in seam allowances, resulting in different block sizes.*

• *Before starting a new project, oil and clean the machine, especially the bobbin case.*

Ironing & Pressing

Unlike pressing, ironing involves a sizable and quick sweeping motion, often with a heavy hand, to remove wrinkles and fold lines.

To press, use a gentle, slow and light-handed technique, usually with the iron tip. When pressing a seam, sewn block or a quilt top, avoid using a distorting side-to-side motion.

Whether one uses a steam or dry iron is of personal preference. Steam-pressing seams create a flatter affect. A travel-size iron is perfect for pressing small areas.

The ironing board needs only minimum padding. The flatter the ironing surface, the more accurate the pressing.

As you sew, it is important to press each seam precisely for more accurate piecing and measuring. Finger pressing, or using a wooden pressing stick, does not provide adequate flattening for miniature-quilt making, except when foundation piecing.

Seams can be pressed either open or together flat to one side. Flat seams are pressed toward the darker fabric. Figure drawings given with each pattern show the direction to press by providing tiny little seams pointing toward the pressing direction. If a drawing is not provided, the instructions provide pressing direction (see Figure 1).

Figure 1

Be very careful when pressing bias edges to avoid distortion or stretching.

Rotary Cutting

All rotary cutting for projects in this book used Omnigrid rotary-cutting rulers—6" x 6" square and 6" x 12" and 3" x 18".

"Measure twice, cut once" is probably the most commonly skipped part of cutting fabric. This is especially important to remember when the only fabric piece available is small, no longer available or perhaps vintage, and must be cut right the first time.

Accurate cutting is an important stepping-stone to a successful miniature quilt, and using rotary-cutting equipment will help ensure this. Use a scaled-down mat size and ruler. Equipment needed for a larger-size project will prove to be unmanageable and may not have the necessary markings needed for miniature-quilt making.

Stay with the same ruler(s) for an entire project for more consistent cutting. When cutting larger pieces into smaller ones, do not pick them up for repositioning. Rather, turn the cutting mat around into its new cutting position.

While many quilters like to quick-cut fabric stacked up to four layers, stack only two layers for truly accurate cutting of very small pieces.

Fight the temptation to cut all the fabric for a project at one time. A misread or changed quilt plan, figures added up wrong when drafting, or a repeated simple wrong cut can add up to unnecessary and discouraging hours of recutting, ripping or resewing.

Rotary-Cutting Tips

• Stand up for more accurate cutting.

• Cut during daylight hours, especially when cutting dark fabrics.

• For an odd strip measurement, rotary-cut a strip of ⅛"-gridded graph paper the width of the cut strip and affix to underside of ruler with clear tape. The paper template is now your cutting guide. Use this same technique for cutting odd-shaped pieces.

• To keep track of small pieces, place them on paper plates and then stack them. Or store them in plastic zipper bags for future sewing.

• Occasionally, take rotary cutter apart and clean out any accumulated debris.

Machine Sewing
You must be able to stitch an accurate ¼" seam allowance with your sewing machine. Adjust your machine as necessary.

Matching Seams
The usual practice of pinning matched seams and then directly sewing the entire seam length is not practical or efficient in miniature-quilt making. It often results in much ripping and resewing, especially with closely spaced seams. However, the "pin and baste" method is ideally suited and results in perfectly matched seams. It is especially helpful when matching more than two seams that meet in one spot.

Tip

• To check for ¼" sewing accuracy, cut three different fabrics each 1½" x 10"; sew the strips together along the length. Press the seams away from the center strip. Place a 1" x 12" C-Thru ruler on the center strip; it should measure 1" wide. Next, measure several times across the sewn strips. This measurement should be 3½" wide. If your measurements do not match these, your sewing machine is not stitching an accurate ¼" seam.

For seams pressed open, position the two pieces right sides together. From one wrong side, place a pin perpendicularly through both seams and ¼" down from top raw edges as shown in Figure 2. Align seams, place a pin on either side of them and remove the first pin. With about 4 or 5 basting stitches per inch, sew across matched seams with ¼"-wide seam allowance. Remove pins and gently open basted area to check for perfect seam alignment as shown in Figure 3. If not, remove basting and start over. Do this for every seam that needs matching along a raw edge.

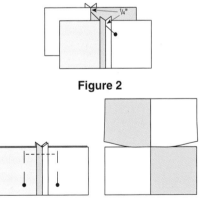

Figure 2

Figure 3

If seams match, pin and sew entire seam length with about 12–14 stitches per inch as shown in Figure 4. Gently remove basting thread.

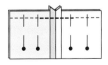

Figure 4

For seams pressed flat to one side, place pieces with right sides together and butt or slide opposing seam allowances together for a tight fit as shown in Figure 5. Repeat the above steps of pinning and basting for seams being pressed open as shown in Figure 6.

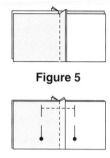

Figure 5

Figure 6

A block having all seams pressed open will be more accurate in size than one having seams pressed to one side. In the latter process, a thread or two are taken up in the seam line, and this adds up quickly in a miniature block.

Trimming Seams

To trim or not is a personal choice, but trimming during assembly does help make a block lie flatter, be more accurate in size and enable easier quilting. However, once a seam or area has been trimmed, it cannot be undone. Therefore, make trimming decisions when making a sample block. Always press first, then trim.

There are two ways to trim. A seam can be trimmed or graded to ⅛"-wide along a seam line to reduce bulk or thickness. For example, if sewing a sashing strip to a pieced block, trim the bulkier block raw edge.

You may want to trim seams to reduce bulk at matching or intersecting seams by trimming off a small triangle across the top of the fabric corners as shown in Figure 7.

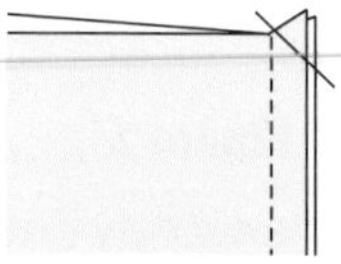

Figure 7

Measuring a Block Accurately

Pattern measurements are perfect dimensions and are not always easy to achieve, especially for very small blocks with many pieces.

Block size can be affected by slight variations in sewing machines, needle and thread size, how precisely fabric was cut and sewn, whether seams were pressed open or flat, and the fabric itself. Any inaccuracy will compound itself, resulting in odd-size blocks that do not match. A block that is a wee bit off-size can be fudged into place. However, if one is way off, it is faster and more accurate to cut and sew a new block.

For accuracy as you sew and press, constantly measure with a 1" x 12" C-Thru ruler to check size. Be prepared to rip, if necessary.

To measure a sewn block accurately, measure the finished-block size in both directions, from inside seam allowance to inside seam allowance as shown in Figure 8. Next, measure the outside block size, which should equal the finished block size plus ¼" seam allowance all around; the block should measure ½" larger than the finished size as shown in Figure 9.

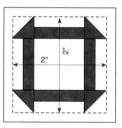

Figure 8

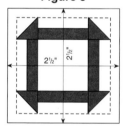

Figure 9

Another way to keep on track is to make a full-size copy of the pattern on a piece of ¼"-gridded plastic template material. Next, make a sample block and position the marked template over the block facing right side up to check for sewing accuracy and help pinpoint trouble spots, referring to Figure 10.

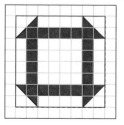

Figure 10

An identical finished-block size helps ensure that everything will fit together, especially if setting blocks side by side and matching their seams. It is OK if the blocks are either all larger or all smaller than the quilt plan, as long as their measurements are consistent. However, you must then make some corresponding mathematical adjustments when cutting other pattern pieces, such as sashings and borders.

Assembly-Line (Chain) Piecing

Assembly-line piecing is a quick-and-easy way to sew up blocks, whether identical or scrap. Place like block pieces in piles next to the sewing machine according to their correct color order and position. After sewing, press them all at once and continue on with more like block pieces in the same fashion until blocks are complete.

Before putting machine needle in fabric, lock threads by making several stitches. After stitching seam, again lock several stitches; then position next piece to be sewn. Repeat locking threads when finished as shown in Figure 11. With this method, block pieces are not butted next to one another, and when locked stitches are cut, the stitched ends of each piece will not come unstitched.

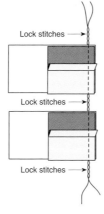

Figure 11

Strip Piecing

Many block patterns are ideally suited for strip piecing. The Nine-Patch is a perfect example; instead of cutting small individual squares, the quick and accurate strip-piecing method is used (Figures 12 and 13).

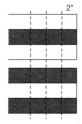
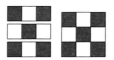

Figure 12   **Figure 13**

Strip piecing is the method by which two or more rotary-cut fabric strips are sewn with right sides together along the length to make a strip set. The strips can be of either equal or unequal widths. After pressing seams, cut pieced segments, which can then be reassembled into blocks, or the strips can be used for sashings or borders.

There are some basic rules of thumb when strip piecing. Find both the lengthwise and crosswise grains of fabric.

When cutting multiple strips, it will occasionally be necessary to square up the long cutting edge of the fabric to keep it on the straight of grain. Tear off a fabric strip along this edge, trim torn edge with rotary equipment, press edge flat, and resume cutting. Also, when cutting many pieced segments from a strip set, it will be necessary to occasionally square up the cutting edge of the strip set with rotary equipment.

Sew strip sets with about 16–18 stitches per inch to avoid stitches coming undone at the edges when pieced segments are cut from a strip set.

To avoid strip-set bowing, reverse the direction in which strips are sewn. That is, sew the first seam from top to bottom, the next from bottom to top and so on. After strips are sewn into a strip set, press seams on both sides, starting with the wrong side, in order to set stitches into the seams. Or if strips are narrow, press each seam after stitching.

An example of a strip-pieced quilt is the Nine-Patch Floral Garden (page 46), which contains strip-pieced sashing and two Nine-Patch sashing blocks.

Bias Squares

Bias squares are triangle-square units or half-square triangle units that are cut from stitched bias squares to result in straight-grain edges. When stitching triangle-square units for miniature-quilt making, the bias-square method results in accurate-size squares no matter the size.

A bias square is made up of two equal-size, right-angle triangles as shown in Figure 14. When cutting the fabric bias strips to be used to make bias squares, it is easiest to work with fabric pieces no larger than 11" x 18" or half of a fat quarter.

Figure 14

Start by making sure that the two fabric pieces required are on the straight of grain. Layer them right sides together, matching one short edge and one long edge of each fabric at a corner. Spray them with fabric spray sizing and iron flat.

Place a 3" x 18" ruler with a 45-degree diagonal line on the matched long fabric edges and make the first cut from the corner as shown in Figure 15. Move the ruler and make a second cut the desired bias strip width, resulting in two matching bias strips as shown in Figure 15.

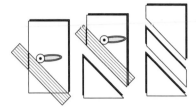

Figure 15

Some of the bias strips may be of different lengths; these may be treated like all other strip sets as shown in Figure 16.

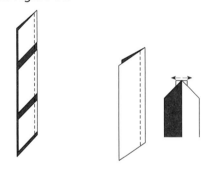

Figure 16   **Figure 17**

Sew bias strips together with 16–18 stitches per inch on one long edge to make a bias set. Gently steam-press seam open, first on the wrong side, and then on right side, referring to Figure 17.

Place the prepared template on the strip with diagonal line on the square template on the stitched lines of the bias strip as shown in Figure 18; cut out shape.

Figure 18

Use a ruler to cut the bias squares. Place the ruler on the strip with the correct-size square at bottom point and cut along edge as shown in Figure 19. The resulting unit will need to be trimmed one more time using the ruler to complete the bias square as shown in Figure 20. Repeat cutting and trimming with the ruler to cut multiple bias squares from one strip.

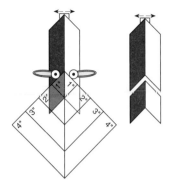

Figure 19

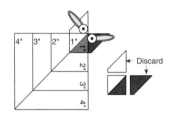

Figure 20

Tips

• *If using a ruler to make bias squares is new to you, make a sample bias set and practice cutting bias squares before using on actual project.*

• *Be sure to have good contrast between the two colors used to make the bias strips.*

• *Cut extra bias strips from leftover fabric and set aside for future projects.*

• *Save any extra bias squares for future miniature scrap quilts.*

Adding Sashing

Sashings, sometimes called lattice, are narrow strips of fabric used to separate either small blocks or blocks having many seams to match. It also expands the size of a quilt and adds visual interest, especially if there is good color separation between sashing and blocks.

Sometimes it is difficult to differentiate between a sashing and a border in a quilt plan, especially when there is more than one sashing. Sashing tends to be narrower than the border and is found in the inner part of the quilt.

Sashing can be sewn on either horizontally or vertically, but it is usually a combination of both. Combined sashing is shown in Fanciful Daisies (page 43).

A strip-pieced sashing is also a bit more complicated. The Nine-Patch Floral Garden (page 46) is the perfect example of this type of sashing.

For something a bit different, simple folded sashing strips may be stitched between the border and the quilt center. Instead of strips, sashing can also be pieced.

Sashing width is usually cut in mathematical proportion to a finished-block size. For example, a ½"-wide finished sashing would be appropriate for a 2½" x 2½" finished block. If in doubt, cut sashing wider than needed, preview it with the blocks and trim down, if necessary.

Sashing strips should be cut on the lengthwise grain of the fabric unless using a print and the fabric design runs along the width.

After sewing, press seams toward the sashing. Seams may be trimmed or graded to reduce bulk.

Squaring Up the Quilt Top

It is always a good idea to measure and square a quilt before adding a border. Start by measuring down both sides of the quilt. These measurements should be identical. Repeat with top and bottom measurements, which should also be identical. If any of the measurements are off more than ⅛", now is the time to examine the quilt for sewing discrepancies and repair, if possible.

If oversized setting triangles are used, it may be necessary to even up the raw edges and square corners. Corners that are not square are very common with diagonally set blocks, and can be made square again by using the corner of a square ruler as a trimming guide.

If a raw edge is uneven, position the top right side up and trim any excess fabric while trying to maintain a ¼"-wide seam allowance and not cut off block points. Next, using a ruler and marking tool, mark on the wrong side of the quilt where the seam allowance should be to serve as a sewing guide.

Borders

Borders frame your quilt. They can be simple fabric strips, pieced designs or appliqué motifs. For miniature quilts, they should not compete with the quilt center.

Some quilters put off choosing border fabric as the last item on their sewing agenda, while others start with a border fabric and build their quilt around it.

Borders can have either butted or straight ends, or have angled, mitered corners. Mitered borders take more time and patience, but add a professional finish, especially if there are lines that must be matched in the fabric used.

To cut side borders, first measure straight down the center of the quilt. If using mitered corners, add twice the border-strip width plus an extra 2". Next, measure the width straight across the center of the quilt for top and bottom border measurements, again adding twice the border-strip width plus an extra 2" if mitering corners.

Cut border fabric on the lengthwise grain of fabric for less stretching. Its width is usually cut in mathematical proportion to the block size. For example, a quilt made with 3½" x 3½" blocks would look good with a border 3½" wide or two borders that combine to 3½". An exception is when one would not want to interrupt or cut into a directional print in order to maintain the fabric design in one piece.

For butted or straight ends, the sewing is simple. Sew sides first, press seams toward borders. Sew top and bottom edges and repeat pressing.

For sewing mitered corner seams, sew a side strip first, stopping stitching on the seam line of the quilt center as shown in Figure 21. Repeat with strip on the opposite side and then the top and bottom strips as shown in Figure 22.

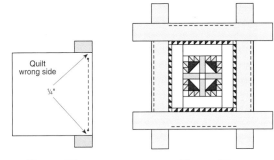

Figure 21   Figure 22

Fold and press the strips at a 45-degree angle to the corner as shown in Figure 23 on page 14. Turn the quilt over; pin strips, matching edges, and stitch along the pressed line from the outside point to the point where stitching border strips ends as shown in Figure 24. Trim seam to ¼" referring to Figure 25; press seam open.

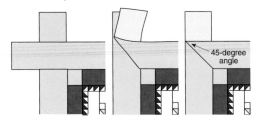

Figure 23

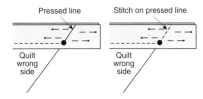

Figure 24

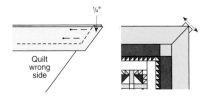

Figure 25

After pressing, turn the quilt to the right side and check each corner to be sure it lies flat. If it does not, rip stitches out carefully and start over.

If mitering a sashing and a border, first join the strips and then sew to the quilt as one edge piece, mitering corners as one and matching seams of strips when sewing corner seams.

Repeating a quilt fabric in the border or border cornerstone is an easy way to tie everything together as shown on Churn Dash Delight (page 53).

For a very busy quilt, a simple border helps to contain the excitement. The Kaleidoscope quilt (page 33) is a perfect example of a busy quilt with a simple border.

Multiple borders can change the dimensions of a quilt, making it square or rectangular. Multiple borders and sashings are also an effective way to surround and accentuate a quilt center.

The right border print can help to continue the theme of the quilt center as is seen on Fanciful Daisies (page 43). Here the flower theme of the blocks is repeated with a floral print in the border. Multiple borders and multiple cornerstones lend

a certain panache to an otherwise ordinary-looking quilt as demonstrated in the Cotton Nights (page 23). Pieced cornerstones can also add flair to the borders.

Keep in mind, not every miniature quilt needs a border to make it complete. The Nine-Patch Floral Garden (page 46) and Log Cabin Pineapple (page 39) quilts would seem too busy with added borders.

Finishing Details
When you have finished sewing the quilt top, steam-press on both sides. Check for proper seam pressing and trim loose threads before preparing to quilt.

Special Techniques
Several of the miniature quilts in this book use special techniques. The following instructions will help you when using the techniques.

Making Yo-Yos
Using the yo-yo circle pattern given with the quilt project, prepare a plastic template. Cut out as directed for the project.

Turn under ¼" around the outside edge of the circle. Knot a single thread and sew short running stitches around the turned-under edge as shown in Figure 1.

Figure 1

When finished stitching, gently pull the thread to draw the circle into a small pouch as shown in Figure 2; knot the thread.

Figure 2

Flatten the pouch into a circle to create a yo-yo as shown in Figure 3.

Figure 3

Yo-yos are commonly used to simulate flowers. They may have uncovered centers or buttons sewn in the centers. These 3-D circles are fun to stitch. Use small fabric scraps to add color and dimension to any quilt, large or small.

Machine Paper-Foundation Piecing

Commonly called the flip-and-sew method, machine-paper foundation piecing is done with numbered fabric pieces. However, for a change, in this book, the seam lines are numbered and the first fabric piece is identified with an X as shown in Figure 4. This will avoid confusion in fabric placement and order of stitching.

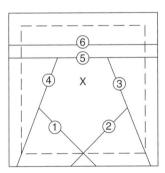

Figure 4

This flip-and-sew method is easy to understand once several fabric pieces are sewn in place. Each block is made with a paper foundation marked with pattern sewing lines that are stitched in numerical order. Although time-consuming, this method results in precise sewing of tiny fabric pieces that can be cut freehand ahead of time. Some finished blocks require mirror-image or reversed parts as shown on Figure 5. Others might require several foundation-pieced units, which are then joined to create the block as shown in Figure 6.

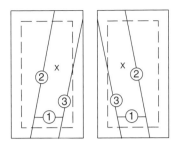

Figure 5

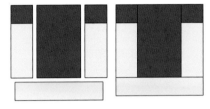

Figure 6

Place tracing paper over the foundation pattern given. Transfer the X, numbered sewing lines and outside ¼"-wide seam allowance using a dark pen or marker, keeping traced copy precise. Duplicate the number of copies required to finish the project. Leave a space between blocks for ease of handling. Cut out patterns leaving a margin around each one.

Choose small-scale prints with good color contrast and close design. Solids work in well. Decide fabric placement before sewing. Repeat fabrics throughout blocks to help tie the blocks together. Highlight smallest block pieces with the brightest or darkest fabrics to make them stand out. If they blend in, they will be lost.

Fabric scraps should be the same size as the pattern piece plus an extra ¼"-wide seam allowance all around, which will be trimmed after sewing. Wrinkled scraps do not need to be ironed in advance. Place directional prints as necessary to create the proper placement in the finished quilt.

Cut triangles from oversized squares. For a more professional look, cut fabric pieces so their grain lines all run in the same direction and on the straight of grain, especially in those pieces on block outside raw edges.

Sew with 16–18 stitches per inch unless thread pulls up on the machine while sewing. Use a neutral-color thread for scrap quilts or matching thread for coordinated color quilts.

Begin and end each seam with 3 or 4 extra stitches beyond the seam lines as shown in Figure 7 on page 16. For identical blocks, sew fabric pieces assembly-line fashion. Before trimming seams, flip fabric pieces right side up to be sure they were sewn in the correct numerical order.

Figure 7

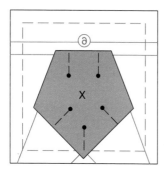

Figure 8

The X or first fabric piece is the only one placed right side up and not flipped over after stitching. To start, hold the paper foundation up to the light for fabric placement, if necessary. Pin or spot-glue fabric piece X in place right side up on unmarked side of the foundation paper as shown in Figure 8.

With right sides together, place fabric piece 1 over piece X as shown in Figure 9; match and trim raw edges ¼" wide along seam 1 line. Sew on seam 1 line; trim raw edges ⅛" wide and flip fabric piece 1 right side up and flat as shown in Figure 10. Finger-press seam and fabric flat.

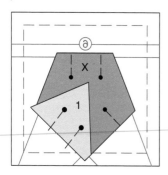

Figure 9

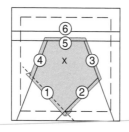

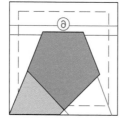

Figure 10

With right sides together, place fabric piece 2 over piece 1; match and trim raw edges ¼" wide along seam 2 line. Sew on seam 2 line; trim raw edges ⅛" wide and flip fabric piece 2 right side up and press flat.

Continue sewing, trimming, flipping and finger-pressing in this manner until all lines are sewn on and the block or unit is complete. Be sure to leave a ¼"-wide seam allowance on block outside raw edge.

If necessary, trim block edges square with rotary equipment. Do not sew outside raw edges flat. Finish quilt top according to instructions. Carefully remove paper foundations with seam-ripper tip. Avoid ripping stitches.

Finishing Your Quilt

Larger projects require much more time during the finishing process. Miniature quilts are easy to manipulate because of their small size, making the finishing process less tedious and more fun.

Marking Top for Hand Quilting

Several basic sewing supplies and tools are required for marking the quilt top for hand quilting.

The proper tool for marking is important. The goal is to mark the top with a design so it is easy to see during the quilting process, but is not visible once the quilt is complete. You may use any of the following marking tools:

• A fine .2mm, hard-lead pencil (soft lead leaves a blurry line)

• Ultimate Marking Pencil for Quilters

• .5mm colored pencils (except red)

• Blue or white fine-point, water-soluble pens

• Quilter's Choice silver or white pencils

• Fabric-pencil eraser

Marking-Pencil Removal

Other supplies include: ¼"-wide quilter's tape, plastic templates, light box and medium-fine sandpaper.

Before you begin, test a scrap of quilt fabric to check for easy marking and complete removal. In most cases, the quilt top should be marked before the layering process. However, some markers do rub off easily during quilting so it may be necessary to mark as you quilt. The use of a thin, lightweight batting makes marking easy even after layering.

Always use a light hand when marking with a pencil. Be sure to remove the marks completely after quilting. If you wait, the marks can become permanent with time.

If using a water-soluble marking pen, soak the finished quilt in cold water since the marking substance could migrate to the batting with simple wiping or spraying.

Quilter's tape is useful when quilting straight lines. Do not leave tape on the quilt surface for long periods of time, especially in a warm climate.

If the fabric is a light color, tape the quilting design to a window and tape the quilt top over the design to mark. A light box works even better than a window, and many inexpensive options are available at your local quilt shop or art-supply store.

If marking the quilt top on a tabletop, place a piece of medium-fine sandpaper under it to prevent slippage.

Many appealing small plastic template designs can be purchased at a quilt shop or through mail-order sources. Be sure they are laser-cut. You may reduce larger-size patterns to fit these small quilts and make your own plastic templates to add to your quilting-design choices.

If you are quilting in the ditch of seams or echo-quilting (repeating a design's shape a certain distance from its edge either inside or outside), you don't need to mark the top. Some fabrics are hard to mark, so these quilting options work best with those types of fabrics.

Choosing Batting

Unlike a full-size quilt, batting requirements for a miniature quilt are quite simple—batting is used for quilting purposes and appearance only, not for warmth. The type of batting chosen is a matter of personal taste and should be appropriate for a particular project. The following are some guidelines to help you choose the right batting for your quilt.

A 100 percent cotton, or 80 percent cotton/20 percent polyester batting, can produce eye-catching results. Both types are easy to quilt through, and they do not slide around during the quilting process. They work similarly to a flannel board used to hold illustrations. The layers stick together naturally. There are many different brands of these battings. Find your preference through trial and error.

There is a difference between different battings in the way they feel, the thickness and pliability.

Using a low-loft polyester batting will result in a quilt with a puffier appearance. Polyester is more difficult to quilt due to slippage, so it must be well secured during layering; however, it is easier to stitch through than cotton. Some polyester battings beard, leaving little white lint pieces on the quilt top. These show up more on darker fabrics.

A high-loft polyester batting is not suitable for use in a miniature quilt. It produces too much loft. You may split this type of batting by peeling off a thin layer, but it results in a very flat and unappealing appearance.

Any cotton batting will produce a quilt with a more traditional look, while a polyester batting conveys a fuller, more contemporary look.

Use a light-color batting, such as natural or white, when making a light-colored quilt, as a dark batting will shadow through. A light-color batting may be used in a dark-color quilt.

Cut batting at least 1" wider all around than the finished quilt-top measurements. This allows for some shrinkage during the quilting process. The extra batting will be trimmed away later when binding is added.

Tips

• Do not use flannel for batting as it is difficult to quilt through and results in a flat look.

• Take care when pressing any type of polyester batting after layering as it might melt.

• Silk batting, although expensive, is easy to quilt through but does result in a somewhat flat look.

• A longer quilting needle is required for quilting through polyester batting.

• If planning to machine-quilt, experiment first with scrap fabric and different battings to find your comfort zone and perfect results for this type of quilting.

House of White Birches, Berne, Indiana 46711   Clotilde.com

Choosing & Preparing Backing

There are several decisions to make when choosing a fabric for the quilt backing. A fabric print that coordinates with or matches the quilt top adds a pleasant and often overlooked finishing touch. This fabric may or may not be used in the quilt top. A matching solid may also be used, but unlike a print, every quilting stitch will be highly visible. A medium-to-large scale or overall print is appropriate. Muslin may be used, but is rather dull.

Cut the backing fabric at least 1½" larger all around than the measurement of the finished quilt top. This allows for some shrinkage during quilting. Larger quilt tops require more backing exposed around outside edges for use when attaching the quilt to a frame and to protect the batting and top edges during the quilting process. These tiny quilts don't require frames, so this excess is not necessary.

Tip

• For a rectangular-shaped quilt, cut backing fabric with its lengthwise straight of grain parallel to the quilt's longer side edges.

Layering the Quilt

The process of layering the batting between the quilt top and backing is often called sandwiching. When the quilt is finished with a bound edge, the layering process requires the batting to be secured between the top and bottom layers.

To layer, place the backing fabric wrong side up and tape to a flat surface along the raw edges. Center the batting on top; center the finished quilt top on the batting layer. **Note:** *You might want to iron the layers together if they do not lie flat. If the quilt top has been marked for quilting, do not iron. Do not iron on a cutting mat.*

There are two ways to secure the layers—pinning or basting. When pinning, use small brass safety pins and start in the quilt center and work out to the edges. The pins may be removed as the areas around them are quilted.

To hand-baste the layers together, use white basting thread, knotting end tails on the quilt top

for easy removal. Begin basting at the quilt center and work to outside edges as shown in Figure 1.

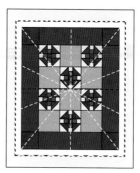

Figure 1

The goal when securing the quilt layers is to keep them from shifting during the quilting process. The shifting could cause lumps, wrinkles and a skewed finished quilt.

Tips

• *Do not pin or baste in the way of future quilting.*

• *Tape backing fabric to a cutting mat that cannot be damaged either by pinning or basting.*

• *Avoid using a colored thread for hand basting, such as red; it can leave a color trail when being pulled out, especially on a light fabric.*

Hand Quilting

Miniature quilts present an excellent opportunity to try out hand quilting. Hand quilting is a way of adding your personal touch to a miniature quilt and gives an air of authenticity.

Needle size and brand are a personal choice. It is a good idea to try several different ones to see how they work for you. The higher the number the finer the needle.

Using a thimble to prevent sore fingers is also a personal choice. A large variety of thimble tools are available from leather to metal.

A quilt frame is not necessary for quilting miniature quilts. If the layers are secure, they will not wrinkle or buckle.

The color and kind of thread to use is also a personal choice. Avoid using one that will be totally lost in the quilt unless you are worried that your stitches are not even or consistent in length. Sink both beginning and ending knots in a seam as you quilt as shown in Figure 2. Hand-quilting threads are available in a variety of colors.

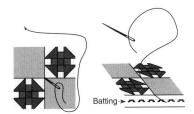

Figure 2

Begin quilting in the center of the quilt and work out to the outer edges. Some quilters like to start at the top and work down. Whatever method you choose, it is best not to add too much quilting. Quilt minimally at first and return to quilt more later, if desired.

As you quilt, turn the work to the back side and check for evenly spaced and sized stitches free of tangles. If a quilt has a border, quilt the inside of blocks first and the borders last.

If you are new to hand quilting, it is more important to strive for evenly sized and spaced stitches than small stitches, which will come with time and practice.

If you like the quilt-in-the-ditch quilting pattern, place small stitches in the seam line between pieces. This is the best type of quilting to use inside very small pieces.

Tips

• *Thread and knot a number of needles ahead of time to speed up quilting time.*

• *If choosing to start quilting in the center of your quilt, cut an extra-long thread and do not knot. Thread needle and use half of the thread from the center to one outside edge; thread needle again with the remaining half of the thread and stitch to the opposite side outside edge. This prevents extra knots in the center of your quilt.*

Outline quilting is done ⅛"–¼" away from a seam line or appliqué design. If repeated several times, it is called echo quilting. The quilting stitches follow the outline of the pieces as shown in Figure 3.

Figure 3

Background quilting fills in large, plain spaces. A common quilting design for this purpose is a crosshatch design in squares or diamonds as shown in Figure 4.

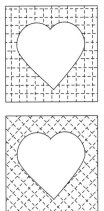

Figure 4

Design quilting includes a variety of designs that add detail to open spaces. Common examples include feather wreaths, clamshells or a braided design as shown in Figure 5.

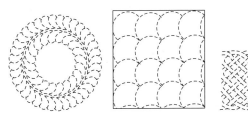

Figure 5

House of White Birches, Berne, Indiana 46711 Clotilde.com

20

The last quilting design is one that you make yourself from ¼" gridded template material. These designs include practically any shape that you can trace around. Hearts and stars are common quilting shapes you can make yourself.

Binding Your Quilt

When the quilting is complete, the edge of the quilt needs to be finished. Begin by trimming the backing and batting edges even and square with the quilted top; remove pins or basting if any still remain. Remove any quilting marks.

Choose binding fabric to match the fabrics used in the quilt to tie the quilt together. This may be a fabric used in blocks or background. To keep it in proportion, the finished binding is ¼"-wide on both the front and back side of the quilt. Larger quilts have a wider binding.

To make binding, cut 1"-wide binding strips on the lengthwise fabric grain, 1⅛"-wide if the fabric is loosely woven. Turn under one long raw edge ¼"; press.

If binding each side with a separate strip, each strip should be cut 1" longer than the measurement of the side to be stitched. Sew a strip to opposite sides of the quilt top with the right side of the strip against the right side of the quilt, matching raw edges as shown in Figure 6.

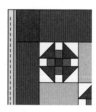

Figure 6

When stitching is complete, turn the binding strips to the back side of the quilt to enclose the quilt edge as shown in Figure 7; hand-stitch in place. Trim ends even with quilt. Repeat with top and bottom strips, leaving ½" excess at each end as shown in Figure 8.

Figure 7

Figure 8

Press strip up and fold in each end as shown in Figure 9; fold to the back side to enclose seam and hand-stitch in place as before. Blind-stitch open ends of seam closed.

Figure 9

If binding all sides with one continuous piece of binding, measure to find total distance around the quilt top edge. Add 6"–8" to the measurement for mitering corners and overlapping beginning and ends.

Cut strips to equal this measurement along the length of the fabric. Cut ends of each strip at a 45-degree angle as shown in Figure 10; join strips to make one long strip. Press seams open and trim to ⅛".

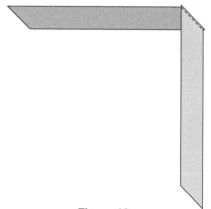

Figure 10

Press under one long edge ¼". Pin strip to quilt with right sides together, starting at least 2" from a corner. Stitch to ¼" from a corner and stop stitching; leave the needle in the quilt, turn and sew diagonally to the corner as shown in Figure 11.

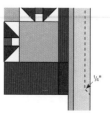

Figure 11

Fold the binding at a 45-degree angle up and away from the quilt as shown in Figure 12 and back down flush with the raw edges. Starting at the top raw edge of the quilt, begin sewing the next side as shown in Figure 13. Repeat at the next three corners.

Figure 12   **Figure 13**

As you approach the beginning of the binding strip, stop stitching and overlap the binding ½" from the edge; trim. Join the two ends with a ¼" seam allowance and press the seam open. Reposition the joined binding along the edge of the quilt and resume stitching to the beginning.

To finish, bring the folded edge of the binding over the raw edges and blind-stitch the binding in place over the machine-stitching line on the back side. Hand-miter the corners on the back as shown in Figure 14.

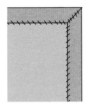

Figure 14

Helpful Hints for Miniature-Quilt Making

• *Before ironing wrinkled or limp fabric, liberally spray it with fabric sizing.*

• *Use the same sewing machine for the entire project for identical seam allowances throughout.*

• *Sew slowly with an accurate and consistent ¼"-wide seam allowance.*

• *Ironing surface should have a minimum of padding for ideal pressing.*

• *Always gently press pieces with iron tip as you sew—no finger-pressing.*

• *If one block is way off in size, it is usually more practical and accurate to make a new block than to rip and resew the off one.*

• *Accentuate small blocks or border pieces by using, for example, your lightest, brightest or darkest fabric for high contrast.*

• *Test dark fabric for dye stability. If it runs, do not use.*

• *Use only high-quality, 100 percent cotton fabric for optimum finished results.*

• *New fabric does not need prewashing. Its sizing agent provides for thread stability and crispness, making it easier and more accurate to cut and sew small pieces.*

• *Cut and paste up, or sew a test block to preview fabric selection and/or check sewing accuracy before cutting fabric and sewing up the entire project.*

• *If possible, coordinate fabric manufactured from the same design line—the thread count is usually identical, making for more manageable work.*

• *Use a fine thread for hand quilting, and strive for evenly spaced, small stitches.*

• *Cut binding strips 1"-wide; 1¹⁄₁₆"-wide for woven fabrics, such as homespun.*

• *Sew the entire seam length—no need to backstitch at the beginning or end of seam.*

House of White Birches, Berne, Indiana 46711   Clotilde.com

Cotton Nights

Pretty pinks and browns combine to make this charming miniature quilt.

Project Specifications
Skill Level: Beginner
Quilt Size: 14¼" x 16½"
Block Size: 2¼" x 2¼"
Number of Blocks: 12

Materials
- 1 fat eighth each pink, black, red check and pink check tonals
- 1 fat eighth each black/white, brown, white/pink and pink prints
- 1 fat quarter each brown stripe, pink/brown squares and black/gray print
- Thin batting 19" x 21"
- Backing 19" x 21"
- Neutral-color all-purpose thread
- Quilting thread
- Basic sewing tools and supplies

Cutting
1. Cut three 2½" x 2½" squares pink check tonal; cut each square in half on one diagonal to make six A triangles.

2. Cut three 2½" x 2½" squares black tonal; cut each square in half on one diagonal to make six B triangles.

3. Cut (12) 2" x 2" squares brown print; cut each square in half on one diagonal to make 24 C triangles.

4. Cut six 2" x 2" D squares red check tonal.

5. Cut (24) 1" x 1" E squares black/white print.

6. Cut four 1" x 21" strips black/white print for binding.

7. Cut (12) ⅞" x 2" F1 strips and (12) ⅞" x 2¾" F2 strips white/pink print.

8. Cut (24) 1¼" x 1¼" G squares pink print.

9. Cut two 1¼" x 9½" H strips and two 1¼" x 8¾" I strips black/gray print.

10. Cut two 1½" x 11" J strips and two 1½" x 10¾" K strips brown stripe.

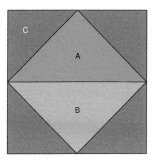

X Block
2¼" x 2¼" Block
Make 6

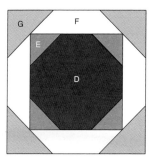

Y Block
2¼" x 2¼" Block
Make 6

11. Cut two 2½" x 13" L strips and two 2½" x 10¾" M strips pink/brown squares print.

12. Cut four 2½" x 2½" N squares pink tonal.

Piecing the X Blocks
Note: *Use ¼" seam allowance; press seams before trimming. Press all seams in the direction of small arrows shown on figure drawings.*

1. To complete one X block, sew A to B along the diagonal as shown in Figure 1; press seam open.

Figure 1

2. Sew a C triangle to each side of the A/B unit to complete one X block as shown in Figure 2; press.

Figure 2

3. Repeat steps 1 and 2 to complete a total of six X blocks.

Piecing the Y Blocks
1. Draw a diagonal line from corner to corner on the wrong side of each E and G square.

2. To complete one Y block, place an E square right sides together on each corner of D and stitch on the marked lines as shown in Figure 3; trim seams to ¼", again referring to Figure 3.

 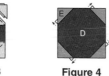

| Figure 3 | Figure 4 | Figure 5 |

3. Press E to the right side to complete a D/E unit as shown in Figure 4.

4. Sew an F1 strip to opposite sides and F2 strips to the remaining sides of the D/E unit as shown in Figure 5; press seams toward F strips.

5. Place a marked G square on each corner of the D/E/F unit and stitch on the marked lines as shown in Figure 6; trim seams to ¼", again referring to Figure 6.

| Figure 6 | Figure 7 |

6. Press G to the right side as shown in Figure 7 to complete one Y block.

7. Repeat steps 2–6 to complete a total of six Y blocks.

Piecing the Top

1. Join one Y block with two X blocks to make an X row as shown in Figure 8; press. Repeat to make two X rows.

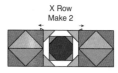 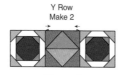

| Figure 8 | Figure 9 |

2. Join one X block with two Y blocks to make a Y row as shown in Figure 9; press. Repeat to make two Y rows.

3. Join the X and Y rows referring to the Placement Diagram for positioning; press seams in one direction.

4. Sew H strips to opposite long sides and I strips to the top and bottom of the pieced center; press seams toward H and I strips.

5. Repeat step 4 with J and K strips; press seams toward J and K.

6. Sew L strips to opposite sides of the pieced center; press seams toward L.

7. Sew an N square to each end of each M strip; press seams toward M.

8. Sew an N-M strip to the top and bottom of the pieced center to complete the quilt top; press seams toward N-M strips.

Finishing

1. Press quilt top on both sides; check for proper seam pressing and trim all loose threads.

2. Mark the top for quilting if using a patterned design. *Note: The quilt shown was hand-quilted with cream thread in the ditch of seams. A single row of quilting is centered in the black and brown borders, and two rows of quilting are centered ½" apart in the pink/brown borders with an X quilted in the corner squares.*

3. Sandwich batting between the stitched top and the backing piece; pin or baste layers together to hold. Quilt as desired by hand or machine.

4. When quilting is complete, trim batting and backing fabric even with raw edges of quilt top.

5. Bind edges with 1"-wide prepared binding strips referring to Binding Your Quilt on page 20. ❖

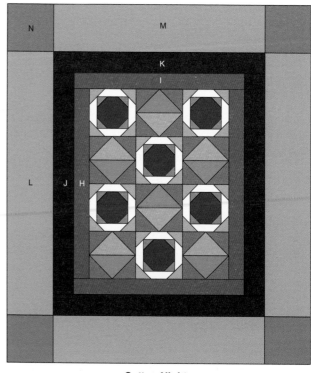

Cotton Nights
Placement Diagram 14¼" x 16½"

Log Cabin Twirler

Use your fabric scraps to create this colorful miniature quilt to brighten any room.

Project Specifications
Skill Level: Beginner
Quilt Size: 15" x 20½"
Block Size: 5½" x 5½"
Number of Blocks: 6

Materials
- 8" x 10" rectangle yellow solid
- 7" x 9" rectangle pink print
- 9" x 10" rectangle turquoise solid
- 7" x 9" rectangle red print
- 9" x 10" rectangle pink solid
- 7" x 18" strip red-and-white print
- 7" x 12" strip dark pink print
- 7" x 7" square dark blue print
- 11" x 18" strip turquoise plaid
- 11" x 18" strip green print
- 1 fat quarter yellow print for binding
- Thin batting 18½" x 24"
- Backing 18½" x 24"
- Neutral-color all-purpose thread
- White quilting thread
- Basic sewing tools and supplies

Cutting
1. Cut (12) 2" x 2" A squares yellow solid.

2. Cut six 2⅜" x 2⅜" B squares pink print.

3. Cut six 2⅜" x 2⅜" C squares, six 1⅛" x 4¾" L strips and six 1⅛" x 6" M strips turquoise plaid.

4. Cut six 1⅛" x 3½" D strips and six 1⅛" x 4¾" E strips turquoise solid.

5. Cut six 2⅜" x 2⅜" F squares, six 1⅛" x 4¾" J strips and six 1⅛" x 6" K strips green print.

6. Cut six 2⅜" x 2⅜" G squares red print.

7. Cut six 1⅛" x 3½" H strips and six 1⅛" x 4¾" I strips pink solid.

8. Cut two 2½" x 17" N strips red-and-white print.

9. Cut two 2½" x 11½" O strips dark pink print.

10. Cut four 2½" x 2½" P squares dark blue print.

11. Cut four 1" x 21" binding strips yellow print.

House of White Birches, Berne, Indiana 46711 Clotilde.com

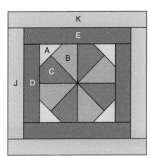

Blue Log Cabin Twirl
5½" x 5½" Block
Make 3

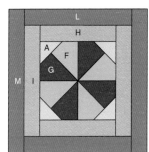

Red Log Cabin Twirl
5½" x 5½" Block
Make 3

Piecing the Blocks
Note: Use ¼" seam allowance; press seams before trimming. Press all seams in the direction of small arrows shown on figure drawings.

1. Cut each B and C square in half on one diagonal to make 12 each B and C triangles.

2. Sew B to C triangle along the diagonal to make a B/C unit as shown in Figure 1; press seam open. Repeat to make a total of 12 B/C units.

Figure 1

3. To make one Blue Log Cabin Twirl block, join two B/C units, reversing one, to make row as shown in Figure 2; press seam open. Repeat to make two rows.

Figure 2

Figure 3

4. Join the two rows to complete one blue unit as shown in Figure 3; press seam to one side.

5. Mark a diagonal line from corner to corner on the wrong side of each A square.

6. Place an A square right sides together on each corner of the blue unit as shown in Figure 4; stitch on the marked line.

Figure 4

Figure 5

7. Trim seams to ¼" and press A to the right side as shown in Figure 5.

8. Sew D strips to opposite sides and E strips to the top and bottom of the blue unit referring to the block drawing; press seams toward D and E strips.

9. Sew J strips to opposite sides and K strips to the top and bottom of the blue unit referring to the block drawing; press seams toward J and K strips to complete one Blue block.

10. Repeat steps 2–9 to complete a total of three Blue blocks.

11. Repeat steps 1–9 with the F and G triangles, A squares and H, I, L and M strips to make a total of three Red blocks.

Piecing the Top

1. Join one Blue block with one Red block to make a block row as shown in Figure 6; press seam toward the Blue block. Repeat to make a total of three rows.

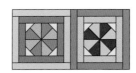

Figure 6

2. Join the rows referring to the Placement Diagram for positioning of rows; press seams in one direction.

3. Sew N strips to opposite long sides of the pieced center; press seams toward strips.

4. Sew a P square to each end of each O strip; press seams toward O.

5. Sew an O-P strip to the top and bottom of the pieced center; press seams toward the O-P strips to complete the quilt top.

Finishing

1. Press quilt top on both sides; check for proper seam pressing and trim all loose threads.

2. Mark the top for quilting as desired. *Note: The quilt shown is hand-quilted with cream thread in the ditch around each block and either cream or turquoise thread in the center of the logs and half-squares.*

3. Sandwich batting between the stitched top and the backing piece; pin or baste layers together to hold. Quilt as desired by hand or machine.

4. When quilting is complete, trim batting and backing fabric even with raw edges of quilt top.

5. Prepare binding using the 1"-wide yellow print strips and bind the quilt edges referring to Binding Your Quilt on page 20. ❖

Log Cabin Twirler
Placement Diagram 15" x 20½"

House of White Birches, Berne, Indiana 46711 Clotilde.com

Amish Bars

This simple quilt is quick and easy to make for a perfect little gift.

Project Specifications
Skill Level: Beginner
Quilt Size: 6½" x 8"

Materials
- 6" x 18" rectangle purple solid
- 10" x 18" rectangle red solid
- 5" x 7" rectangle turquoise solid
- 1 fat quarter black solid for binding
- Thin batting 9" x 11"
- Backing 9" x 11"
- Neutral-color all-purpose thread
- Quilting thread
- Basic sewing tools and supplies

Cutting
1. Cut four 1" x 5½" A strips purple solid.

2. Cut four 1¾" x 1¾" G squares purple solid.

3. Cut three 1" x 5½" B strips red solid.

4. Cut two 1¾" x 6" E strips and two 1¾" x 4½" F strips red solid.

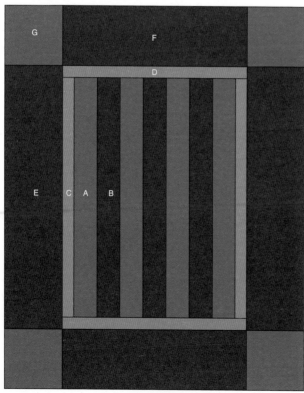

Amish Bars
Placement Diagram 6½" x 8"

5. Cut two ¾" x 5½" C strips and two ¾" x 4½" D strips turquoise solid.

6. Cut four 1" x 18" strips black solid for binding.

Piecing the Top
Note: *Use ¼" seam allowance; press seams before trimming. Press all seams in the direction of small arrows shown on figure drawings.*

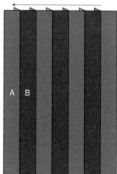

Figure 1

1. Alternate and join four A strips and three B strips as shown in Figure 1; press.

2. Sew a C strip to opposite long sides and D strips to the top and bottom of the A/B center; press seams toward C and D strips.

3. Sew E strips to opposite long sides of the quilt center; press seams toward E.

4. Sew a G square to each end of each F strip; press seams away from G.

5. Sew an F/G strip to the top and bottom of the pieced center to complete the pieced top.

Finishing
1. Press quilt top on both sides; check for proper seam pressing and trim all loose threads.

2. Mark the top for quilting if using a patterned design. **Note:** *The quilt shown is hand-quilted in the ditch of center bar seams, with X patterns in corner squares and border F pieces and with a V pattern in border E pieces.*

3. Sandwich batting between the stitched top and the backing piece; pin or baste layers together to hold. Quilt as desired by hand or machine.

4. When quilting is complete, trim batting and backing fabric even with raw edges of quilt top.

5. Join the 1"-wide black solid binding strips with diagonal seams to make one long strip and bind the quilt edges referring to Binding Your Quilt on page 20. ❖

Fans

The flip-and-sew method was used to make the angled fan sections on the tiny fan blocks.

Fan
3" x 3" Block
Make 6

Project Specifications
Skill Level: Beginner
Quilt Size: 14" x 18¼"
Block Size: 3" x 3"
Number of Blocks: 6

Materials
- 8" x 10" rectangle each 6 different fabrics for pieces A–F
- 4" x 9" rectangle purple print
- 8" x 8" square floral print
- 12" x 14" rectangle mauve print
- 14" x 15" rectangle red print
- ⅛ yard pink solid for binding
- 16" x 20½" lightweight batting
- 17" x 21½" backing
- Neutral-color all-purpose thread
- White quilting thread
- Basic sewing tools and supplies

Cutting
1. Cut three 2⅜" x 2⅜" purple print squares. Cut each square in half on one diagonal as shown in Figure 1 to make six G triangles.

Figure 1

2. Cut two 5½" x 5½" H squares, two 3½" x 3½" I squares and two 3" x 3" J squares mauve print. Cut each H square in half on both diagonals as shown in Figure 2 to make eight H triangles. Cut each J square in half on one diagonal as shown in Figure 3 to make four J triangles.

Figure 2

Figure 3

3. Cut two 3" x 13¼" K strips and two 3" x 9" L strips red print.

4. Cut four 3" x 3" M floral print squares.

5. Cut 1"-wide strips pink solid and join to create a 73" binding strip referring to Binding Your Quilt on page 20.

Piecing Blocks
Note: Use a ¼" seam allowance; press seams before trimming. Press all seams in the direction of small arrows shown on figure drawings.

1. Make six copies of the paper-piecing pattern. Prepare fabric pieces and complete six fan units referring to Machine Paper-Foundation Piecing on page 15.

2. Stitch a G triangle to the corner of each fan unit as shown in Figure 4; trim excess layers away from underneath G to complete six Fan blocks.

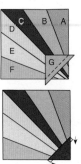

Figure 4

Piecing the Top

1. Arrange the Fan blocks with H, I and J as shown in Figure 5; join in diagonal rows. Join rows and add J to corners, again referring to Figure 5 for positioning; press seams in one direction. Remove paper backing from blocks.

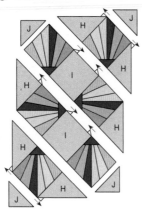

Figure 5

Fans
Placement Diagram 14" x 18¼"

2. Sew L to the top and bottom of the pieced center; press seams toward L.

3. Sew an M square to each end of each K strip; press seams toward M. Sew a K/M strip to opposite long sides of the pieced center; press seams toward K/M.

Finishing

1. Press quilt top on both sides; check for proper seam pressing and trim all loose threads.

2. Mark top for quilting. ***Note:*** *The quilt shown was hand-quilted through the center of each fan piece, in the ditch of seams and in an echo of the fan block in the setting pieces and borders using white quilting thread.*

3. Sandwich batting between the stitched top and the backing piece; pin or baste layers together to hold. Quilt as desired by hand or machine.

4. When quilting is complete, trim batting and backing fabric even with raw edges of quilt top.

5. Bind edges with 1"-wide pink solid prepared binding strips referring to Binding Your Quilt on page 20. ❖

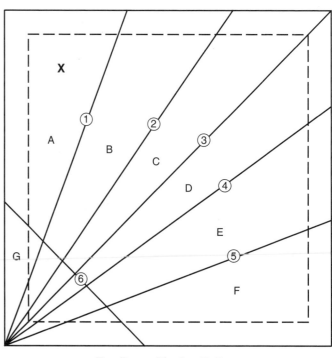

Fan Paper-Piecing Pattern
Make 6 copies

Kaleidoscope

The Kaleidoscope design can be made in planned color patterns or in a scrappy style like the one shown. Its versatility makes it a fun design for playing with fabrics.

Project Specifications
Skill Level: Beginner
Quilt Size: 13" x 15⅛"
Block Size: 2⅛" x 2⅛"
Number of Blocks: 20

Materials
- 80 dark scrap 2½" x 2½" squares for D
- 80 light scrap 2½" x 2½" squares for L
- ½ fat quarter hot pink print
- ½ fat quarter turquoise print
- ⅛ yard blue print for binding
- 15" x 17" lightweight batting
- 16" x 18" backing
- Neutral-color all-purpose thread
- Pink and blue quilting thread
- Basic sewing tools and supplies

Cutting
1. Cut 40 squares 1½" x 1½" hot pink print. Cut each square in half on one diagonal to make A triangles as shown in Figure 1; you will need 80 A triangles.

Figure 1

2. Cut two 2½" x 11⅛" B strips and two 2½" x 13" C strips turquoise print.

3. Cut 1"-wide strips blue print and join to create a 64" binding strip referring to Binding Your Quilt on page 20.

Piecing Blocks
***Note:** Use a ¼" seam allowance; press seams before trimming. Press all seams in the direction of small arrows shown on figure drawings.*

1. Refer to Machine Paper-Foundation Piecing on page 15 for tracing and sewing instructions.

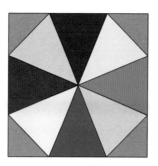

X Block
2⅛" x 2⅛" Block
Make 10

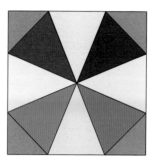

Y Block
2⅛" x 2⅛" Block
Make 10

2. Trace 20 copies each E and F sections using patterns given; complete each section using A triangles for corners and light (L) and dark (D) scraps as indicated on patterns.

3. Join two E sections, referring to Figure 2, to complete one X block; join two F sections to complete one Y block, again referring to Figure 2. Repeat for 10 blocks each X and Y.

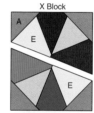

Figure 2

Piecing the Top
1. Join four blocks to make a row, alternating X and Y blocks to make rows, referring to Figure 3. Make three M and two N rows.

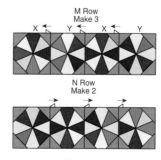

Figure 3

House of White Birches, Berne, Indiana 46711 Clotilde.com

2. Join the M and N rows, alternating rows as shown in Figure 4.

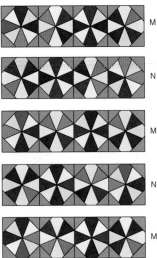

M

N

M

N

M

Figure 4

3. Sew B strips to opposite sides of the pieced center; press seams toward B.

4. Sew C strips to the top and bottom of the pieced center; press seams toward C. Remove paper patterns.

Finishing

1. Press quilt top on both sides; check for proper seam pressing and trim all loose threads.

2. Mark top for quilting using border design given on B and C strips. *Note: The quilt shown was hand-quilted*

through the center of each block in vertical and horizontal rows using pink quilting thread and on the marked lines on B and C borders using blue quilting thread.

3. Sandwich batting between the stitched top and the backing piece; pin or baste layers together to hold. Quilt as desired by hand or machine.

4. When quilting is complete, trim batting and backing fabric even with raw edges of quilt top.

5. Bind edges with 1"-wide blue print prepared binding strips referring to Binding Your Quilt on page 20. ❖

Kaleidoscope
Placement Diagram 13" x 15⅛"

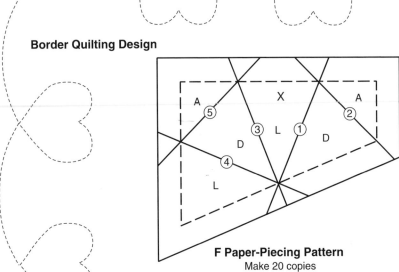

Border Quilting Design

F Paper-Piecing Pattern
Make 20 copies

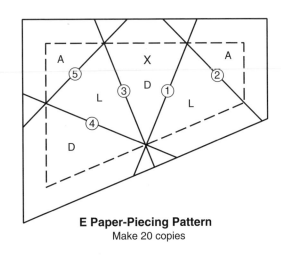

E Paper-Piecing Pattern
Make 20 copies

Charming Log Cabin

Stitch this log cabin mini using paper-pieced patterns for perfect results.

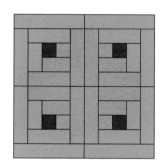

Log Cabin
5" x 5" Block
Make 6

Project Specifications
Skill Level: Beginner
Quilt Size: 14½" x 19½"
Block Size: 5" x 5"
Number of Blocks: 6

Materials
- 6" x 7" scrap red solid
- 7" x 7" square light print
- 10" x 18" rectangle each six assorted light prints
- 10" x 18" rectangle each six assorted medium prints
- 13" x 18" rectangle blue solid
- 1 fat quarter light blue print for binding
- Thin batting 17" x 22"
- Backing 17" x 22"
- Neutral-color all-purpose thread
- Quilting thread
- Basic sewing tools and supplies

Cutting
1. Cut (24) 1" x 1" squares red solid for piece 1.

2. Cut 1"-wide strips from the six assorted light prints for pieces 2, 3, 6 and 7.

3. Cut 1"-wide strips from the six assorted medium prints for pieces 4, 5, 8 and 9.

4. Cut two 2¾" x 15½" C strips and two 2¾" x 10½" D strips blue solid.

5. Cut four 2¾" x 2¾" E squares light print.

6. Cut four 1" x 21" strips light blue print for binding.

Completing the Blocks
Note: Use ¼" seam allowance; press seams before trimming. Press all seams in the direction of small arrows shown on figure drawings. Paper-piecing patterns for A and B units are found on page 62.

1. Refer to Machine Paper-Foundation Piecing on page 15 for tracing and sewing instructions.

2. Complete two A units each having the same light fabric for pieces 2, 3, 6 and 7 and the same medium fabric for pieces 4, 5, 8 and 9 for each block as shown in Figure 1. Repeat for two B units again

referring to Figure 1. *Note: The B units are reversed or mirror images of the A units. You need two A and two B units per block, using the same light and medium fabrics in all A and B units.*

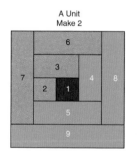
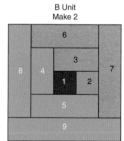

Figure 1

3. Select two each matching mirror-image A and B units; join one each A and B unit to make a row as shown in Figure 2. Repeat to make two rows; press seams in rows in opposite directions.

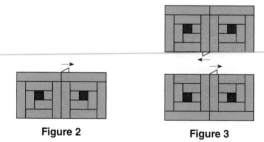

Figure 2   **Figure 3**

4. Join the two rows to complete one Log Cabin block as shown in Figure 3; press seam to one side.

5. Repeat steps 2–4 to complete a total of six Log Cabin blocks.

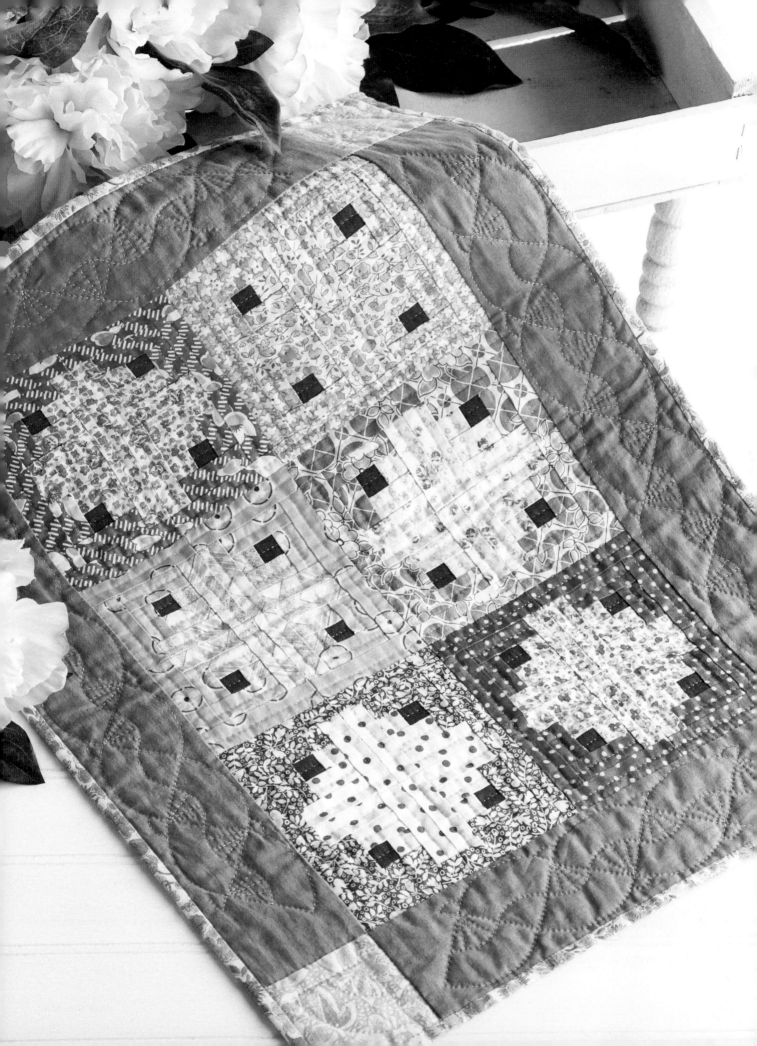

Piecing the Top

1. Arrange and join three Log Cabin blocks as shown in Figure 4 to make a vertical row; press seams in one direction. Repeat to make a second vertical row.

2. Join the two vertical rows with seams in opposite directions to complete the pieced center; press seam to one side.

3. Sew a C strip to opposite long sides of the pieced center; press seams toward C strips.

4. Sew an E square to each end of each D strip; press seams toward D.

5. Sew a D/E strip to the top and bottom of the pieced center to complete the pieced top; press seams toward D/E strips.

6. Using the tip of a seam ripper, carefully remove paper foundations from the back side of each block, making sure not to rip out any stitches.

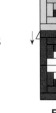

Figure 4

Finishing

1. Press quilt top on both sides; check for proper seam pressing and trim all loose threads.

2. Mark the top for quilting if using a patterned design. *Note: The quilting design given was used in the C and D border strips and in the E border square as shown in Figure 5. A single line of quilting is done through each log and quilting in the ditch around each block.*

Figure 5

3. Sandwich batting between the stitched top and the backing piece; pin or baste layers together to hold. Quilt as desired by hand or machine.

4. When quilting is complete, trim batting and backing fabric even with raw edges of quilt top.

5. Join the 1"-wide light blue print binding strips with diagonal seams to make one long strip and bind the quilt edges referring to Binding Your Quilt on page 20. ❖

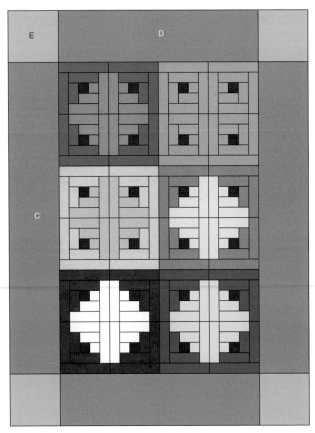

Charming Log Cabin
Placement Diagram 14½" x 19½"

Border Quilting Design

Log Cabin Pineapple

Choose a different color for each pineapple block to create this simple mini.

Project Specifications

Skill Level: Beginner
Quilt Size: 13½" x 13½"
Block Size: 4½" x 4½"
Number of Blocks: 9

Materials

- 1 fat quarter coordinating print for binding
- ⅓ yard total of 9 assorted prints
- ¼ yard white solid
- Thin batting 16" x 16"
- Backing 16" x 16"
- Neutral-color all-purpose thread
- White quilting thread
- Basic sewing tools and supplies

Cutting

1. Cut two 2¾" by fabric width strips white solid; subcut strips into (18) 2¾" B squares and nine 2" x 2" A squares. Cut each B square in half on one diagonal to make 36 B triangles.

2. Cut the remainder of the white solid into 1" by fabric width strips for pieces 5, 6, 7, 8, 13, 14, 15 and 16.

3. Cut each of the nine prints into 1" by fabric width strips for pieces 1, 2, 3, 4, 9, 10, 11, 12, 17, 18, 19 and 20.

4. Cut four 1" x 21" strips coordinating print for binding. Join with diagonal seams to make a long strip.

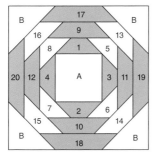

Log Cabin Pineapple
4½" x 4½" Block
Make 9

Piecing the Blocks

1. Trace nine copies of the paper-piecing pattern using pattern given.

2. Using A squares for the center, and B triangles for the outer corners, complete nine Log Cabin Pineapple blocks referring to Machine Paper-Foundation Piecing on page 15.

Completing the Top

1. Select and join three Log Cabin Pineapple blocks to make a row; press seams in one direction. Repeat to make three rows.

2. Join the rows to complete the quilt top, alternating pressing of seam allowances to reduce bulk; press seams in one direction.

3. Using the tip of a seam ripper, carefully remove paper foundations from the back side of each block, making sure not to rip out any stitches.

Log Cabin Pineapple
Placement Diagram 13½" x 13½"

Finishing

1. Press quilt top on both sides; check for proper seam pressing and trim all loose threads.

2. Mark the top for quilting using a patterned design. *Note: The quilt shown was hand-quilted with white thread in an all-over concentric half-circle pattern.*

3. Sandwich batting between the stitched top and the backing piece; pin or baste layers together to hold. Quilt as desired by hand or machine.

4. When quilting is complete, trim batting and backing fabric even with raw edges of quilt top.

5. Bind edges with 1"-wide prepared binding strips referring to Binding Your Quilt on page 20. ❖

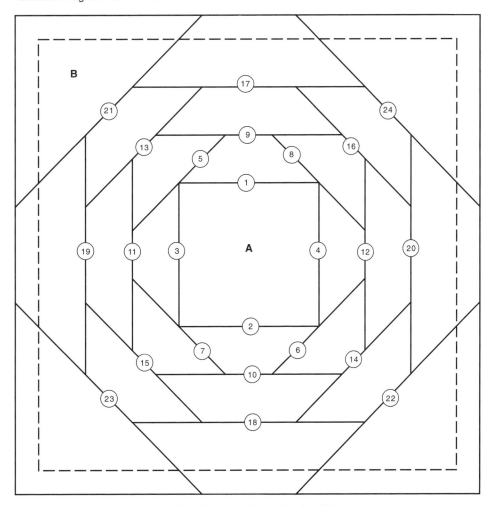

Log Cabin Pineapple Paper-Piecing Pattern
Make 9 copies

Fanciful Daisies

Vintage-fabric appliquéd daisy petals and yo-yo flower centers make a perfect mood-setting little quilt.

Project Specifications
Skill Level: Beginner
Quilt Size: 18¼" x 18¼"
Block Size: 5½" x 5½"
Number of Blocks: 4

Materials
- 32 assorted scraps 2" x 3½"
- 3" x 3" square dark green solid
- 14" x 14" square muslin
- 12" x 14" rectangle pink solid
- ½ fat quarter orange solid
- 14" x 16" rectangle green print
- 7" x 7" square peach print
- ⅛ yard green solid for binding
- 20" x 20" lightweight batting
- 21" x 21" backing
- Neutral-color all-purpose thread
- Cream quilting thread
- ½ yard HeatnBond Lite iron-on adhesive
- Basic sewing tools and supplies, white paper, paper scissors, removable fabric marker

Cutting
1. Prepare template for the A petal using the full-size pattern given; reverse template and trace 32 A pieces on the paper side of the iron-on adhesive. Cut out shapes, leaving a margin around each one. Fuse shapes to the wrong side of the 2" x 3½" assorted scrap pieces.

2. Cut out A shapes on traced lines; remove paper backing.

3. Cut a 3" x 3" square iron-on adhesive; fuse to the wrong side of the 3" x 3" square dark green solid. Trace and cut four B stem pieces on the paper side of the fused square; cut out B on the traced lines. Remove paper backing.

4. Cut four 6" x 6" C squares muslin.

5. Cut six 1¼" x 6" D strips and two 5" x 6" E strips pink solid.

6. Cut three 1¼" x 5" F strips and four G circles orange solid.

Daisy
5½" x 5½" Block
Make 4

7. Cut four 2¾" x 13¾" H strips green print.

8. Cut four 2¾" x 2¾" I squares peach print.

9. Cut 1"-wide strips green solid and join to create an 81" binding strip referring to Binding Your Quilt on page 20.

Appliquéing Blocks
Note: Use a ¼" seam allowance; press seams before trimming. Press all seams in the direction of small arrows shown on figure drawings.

1. Trace the full-size pattern onto a piece of paper.

2. Fold and crease C squares to find the center as shown in Figure 1.

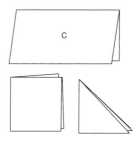

Figure 1

3. Center a C square on the traced paper pattern; transfer design to fabric using a removable fabric marker.

4. Place one B stem piece on a C square on the marked lines for B as shown in Figure 2; fuse in place.

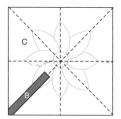

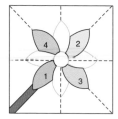

Figure 2   **Figure 3**

5. Arrange A shapes in place, beginning with four A pieces at each diagonal crease line as shown in Figure 3.

6. Arrange remaining A shapes in place, matching their points with folds in C square as shown in Figure 4; when satisfied with positioning, fuse in place. Repeat for four block units. ***Note:*** *When pressing petal shapes in place, always match bottom curved edge of each one with circle edge.*

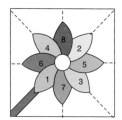

Figure 4

7. Make yo-yos using G pieces referring to Making Yo-Yos on page 14. Center a G yo-yo on a block unit; hand-stitch in place to complete a block; repeat for four blocks.

Piecing the Top

1. Join two blocks with three D strips to make a block row as shown in Figure 5; repeat for two block rows.

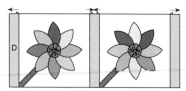

Figure 5

2. Join three F and two E strips with right sides together along length referring to Figure 6 for positioning of strips; press. Subcut strip set into three 1¼" segments, again referring to Figure 6.

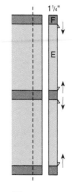

Figure 6

3. Join the block rows with the E-F segments as shown in Figure 7; press.

Figure 7

4. Sew an H strip to two opposite sides of the pieced center; press seams toward strips.

5. Sew an I square to each end of each remaining H strip; press seams toward I. Sew the H-I strips to the remaining sides of the pieced center to complete the top; press seams toward strips.

Finishing

1. Press quilt top on both sides; check for proper seam pressing and trim all loose threads.

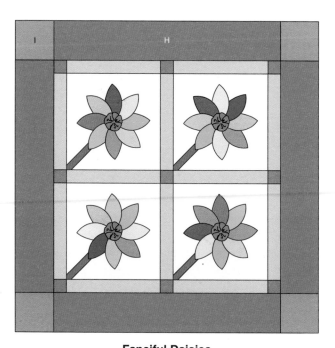

Fanciful Daisies
Placement Diagram 18¼" x 18¼"

2. Mark top for quilting. *Note: The quilt shown was hand-quilted in an echo design around flower motifs, in the ditch of seams and in an X pattern in the F squares using cream quilting thread.*

3. Sandwich batting between the stitched top and the backing piece; pin or baste layers together to hold. Quilt as desired by hand or machine.

4. When quilting is complete, trim batting and backing fabric even with raw edges of quilt top.

5. Bind edges with 1"-wide green solid prepared binding strips referring to Binding Your Quilt on page 20. ❖

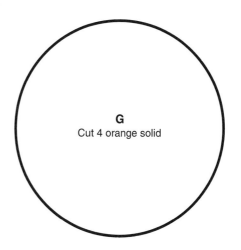

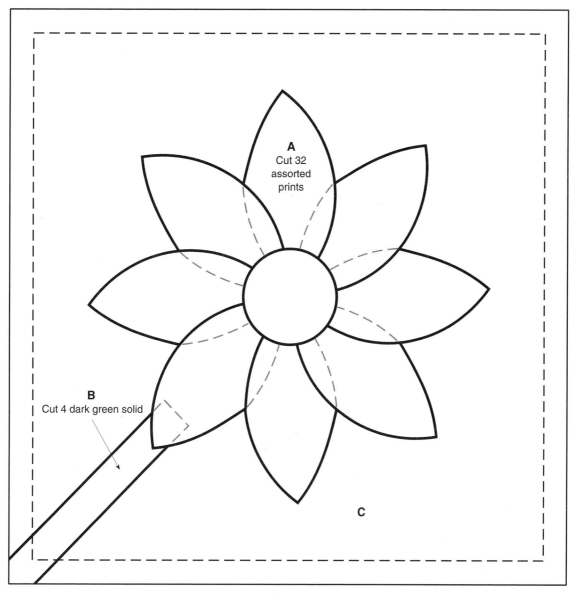

Full-Size Pattern
Trace on paper

House of White Birches, Berne, Indiana 46711 Clotilde.com

Nine-Patch Floral Garden

Made entirely with 1930s and 1940s vintage fabrics, this colorful quilt evokes thoughts of springtime.

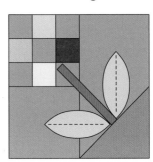

Nine-Patch Floral
4½" x 4½" Block
Make 6

Project Specifications
Skill Level: Advanced
Quilt Size: 11¾" x 18½"
Block Size: 4½" x 4½"
Number of Blocks: 6

Materials
- 3" x 3" squares 6 assorted prints for yo-yos
- 3" x 9" rectangles of 4 assorted floral prints
- 4" x 12" rectangle dark green solid
- 7" x 10" rectangle violet solid
- 8" x 14" rectangle light green solid for G
- 12" x 17" rectangle peach solid
- ½ fat quarter rust solid
- Fat quarter blue solid
- ⅛ yard blue print for binding
- Backing 14" x 21"
- Batting 13" x 20"
- Neutral-color all-purpose thread
- White quilting thread
- Pink and light green 6-strand embroidery floss
- 6 (⅜") orange buttons
- Freezer paper
- Basic sewing tools and supplies

Cutting
1. Cut one 1¼" x 9" A strip from each assorted floral print.

2. Cut five 1¼" x 9" B strips, six 2¾" x 2¾" C squares and six 2¾" x 5" D rectangles blue solid.

3. Cut two 1" x 12" E strips dark green solid.

4. Cut six 2¾" x 2¾" F squares violet solid.

5. Cut six 1¼" x 17" H strips and three 1¼" x 7" J strips peach solid.

6. Cut three 1¼" x 17" I strips and three 1¼" x 7" K strips rust solid.

7. Cut 1"-wide strips blue print and join to create a 69" binding strip referring to Binding Your Quilt on page 20.

Piecing & Appliquéing Blocks
Note: *Use a ¼" seam allowance; press all seams in the direction of small arrows shown on figure drawings.*

1. Sew one A strip between two B strips with right sides together along length as shown in Figure 1; repeat for two strip sets.

2. Subcut each strip set into 1¼" segments, again referring to Figure 1; you will need 12 B/A/B segments.

Figure 1

3. Referring to Figure 2, sew a B strip between two A strips with right sides together along length; subcut strip set into six 1¼" A/B/A segments.

Figure 2   **Figure 3**

4. Join two B/A/B segments with one A/B/A segment to make a Nine-Patch unit as shown in Figure 3; repeat for six Nine-Patch units.

5. Sew C to a Nine-Patch unit and add D to make an X unit as shown in Figure 4 on page 48; repeat for three X units. Repeat to make three Y units referring to Figure 5 on page 48.

Figure 4   Figure 5

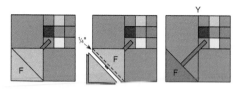

Figure 11

Figure 12

6. Fold one E strip in half along length with wrong sides together; stitch with a scant ¼" seam allowance to make a tube; repeat for two tubes. Trim seams to ⅛" as shown in Figure 6.

Figure 6

7. Referring to Figure 7, rotate seams to the center of each tube; press. Cut each tube into three 3½" lengths for stems.

Figure 7

8. Trim one end of each tube to a point and fold it under as shown in Figure 8.

Figure 8

9. Center each E stem strip diagonally on each X and Y unit and into the first square of the Nine-Patch units as shown in Figure 9.

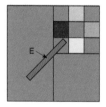

Figure 9   Figure 10

10. Using 2 strands of pink embroidery floss, secure stem pieces in place with small, even overcast stitches as shown in Figure 10.

11. Draw a diagonal line from corner to corner on the wrong side of each F square. Place a square right sides together on the corner of D of each Y block. Stitch on the marked line and trim seam allowance to ¼" as shown in Figure 11; press F open. Repeat on the right corner of each X block referring to Figure 12.

12. Trace 12 leaf shapes on the paper side of the freezer paper using the pattern given. Iron the waxy side of the freezer paper to the wrong side of the light green solid G fabric.

13. Cut out leaf shapes, leaving a ⅛" seam allowance all around when cutting.

14. With paper side up and using the tip of the iron, press seam allowance on each leaf shape toward paper referring to Figure 13.

Figure 13

15. Remove paper from each leaf shape. Pin or baste two leaves to each block referring to the block drawing for placement. Hand-stitch each shape in place using 2 strands of light green embroidery floss and a running stitch. Come up near the tip of each leaf and make one long stitch to the opposite tip; outline-stitch over the floss as shown in Figure 14 to complete blocks. *Note: Yo-yos and buttons are added after quilting.*

Figure 14

Piecing the Top

1. Referring to Figure 15, sew an I strip between two H strips with right sides together along length; repeat for three strip sets. Subcut strip sets into seven 5" segments.

Figure 15

2. Referring to Figure 16, sew a J strip between two K strips with right sides together along length; subcut strip set into four 1¼" segments. Sew a K strip between two J strips; subcut strip set into two 1¼" segments, again referring to Figure 16.

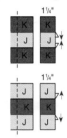

Figure 16

Figure 17

3. Sew a J/K/J segment between two K/J/K segments as shown in Figure 17; repeat.

4. Join two H/I/H units with one J/K unit to make a sashing row as shown in Figure 18; repeat for two sashing rows.

Figure 18

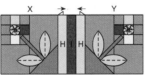

Figure 19

5. Join one each X and Y block with one H/I/H unit to make a block row as shown in Figure 19; repeat for three block rows.

6. Join the block rows with the sashing rows to complete the pieced center referring to the Placement Diagram. Press seams toward sashing rows.

Finishing

1. Press quilt top on both sides; check for proper seam pressing and trim all loose threads.

2. Mark top for quilting. *Note: The quilt shown was hand-quilted in the ditch of seams, through the center of the rust and peach solid strips, and with an X through the center of the sashing Nine-Patch units using white quilting thread.*

3. Sandwich batting between the stitched top and the backing piece; pin or baste layers together to hold. Quilt as desired by hand or machine.

4. When quilting is complete, trim batting and backing fabric even with raw edges of quilt top.

5. Bind edges with 1"-wide blue print prepared binding strips referring to Binding Your Quilt on page 20.

6. Prepare six yo-yos using pattern given and referring to Making Yo-Yos on page 14.

7. Center a yo-yo in each block Nine-Patch unit; hand-stitch in place. Sew a ⅜" orange button in the center of each yo-yo to finish. ❖

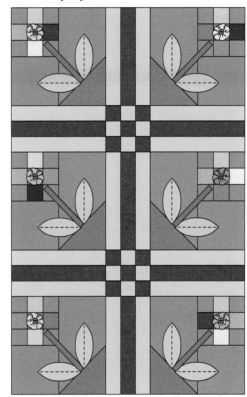

Nine-Patch Floral Garden
Placement Diagram 11¾" x 18½"

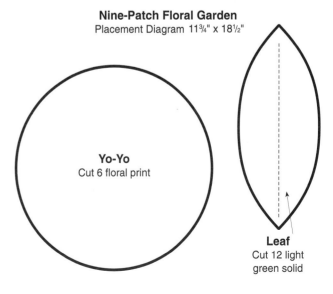

Yo-Yo
Cut 6 floral print

Leaf
Cut 12 light green solid

Spools Variation

A variety of scraps are used in this variation of an old favorite pattern.

Project Specifications
Skill Level: Intermediate
Quilt Size: 10" x 12" (without prairie points)
Block Size: 2" x 2"
Number of Blocks: 12

Materials
- Fat quarter blue print for A
- 6" x 10" rectangle each yellow, brown, black and green prints for B
- 12" x 12" square brown floral for borders
- Fat quarter light green print for H prairie points
- Backing 12" x 14"
- Batting 12" x 14"
- Neutral-color all-purpose thread
- White quilting thread
- Basic sewing tools and supplies, Quilter's Rule Mini Triangle 45-degree ruler

Cutting
1. Cut (12) 1" x 10" A strips blue print.

2. Cut three 1" x 10" B strips each yellow, brown, black and green prints.

3. Cut two 2½" x 8½" F strips and two 2½" x 10½" G strips brown floral.

4. Cut (44) 1½" x 1½" H squares light green print.

Piecing Blocks
Note: Use ¼" seam allowance; press seams before trimming. Press all seams in the direction of small arrows shown on figure drawings.

1. Sew one A strip to each B strip to make an A/B strip set as shown in Figure 1; repeat for three strip sets of each combination.

Figure 1

2. Prepare template for A/B using pattern given. *Note: Pattern given includes a ¼" seam allowance.* Cut four A/B units, alternating placement of A as shown in Figure 2. *Note: If using the Quilter's Rule Mini*

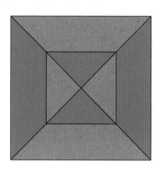

Spools Variation
2" x 2" Block
Make 12

Triangle 45-degree ruler, cut length along long edge 3¼" referring to Figure 2.

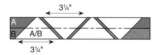

Figure 2

3. Join two matching-color A/B units, alternating placement as shown in Figure 3; repeat for all A/B units.

Figure 3   **Figure 4**

4. Join two matching-color units to complete one block as shown in Figure 4; repeat for 12 blocks.

Piecing the Top
1. Join three blocks to complete an X row, referring to Figure 5; repeat for two X rows. Repeat with remaining blocks to complete two Y rows.

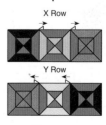

X Row

Y Row

Figure 5

2. Join the rows, alternating X and Y rows as shown in Figure 6 to complete the quilt center.

3. Sew F to opposite long sides and G to the top and bottom of the pieced center; press seams toward F and G.

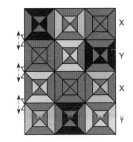

Figure 6

Finishing

1. Press quilt top on both sides; check for proper seam pressing and trim all loose threads.

2. Mark top for quilting if using patterned design. *Note: The quilt shown was hand-quilted ¼" from A/B seams and straight through the border center using white quilting thread.*

3. Referring to Figure 7 to make prairie points, fold each H square in half on one diagonal with wrong sides together; fold again and press. Repeat to make 44 prairie points.

Figure 7

4. Stack all H prairie points with folds in the same direction. Arrange 12 H prairie points along each long side edge as shown in Figure 8, beginning ¼" from quilt corner and overlapping edges at the seam allowance ¼" as shown in Figure 9; baste in place to hold. Stitch in place with a ¼" seam allowance.

Figure 8

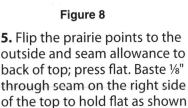

Figure 9

5. Flip the prairie points to the outside and seam allowance to back of top; press flat. Baste ⅛" through seam on the right side of the top to hold flat as shown in Figure 10.

6. Repeat on the top and bottom edges with 10 H prairie points.

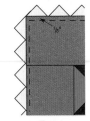

Figure 10

7. Lay backing and batting on the completed top; excluding the prairie points, trim the batting to the exact same size as the quilt top and trim the backing ¼" larger than the quilt top all around.

8. Press under backing edges ¼" all around; place right side down on a flat surface. Place batting inside folded-under seam allowance edges of backing and the completed top on the batting; baste around edges to hold.

9. Hand-stitch backing in place all around, covering seams of prairie points as you stitch. Remove all basting.

10. Quilt on marked lines or as desired to complete the quilt. ❖

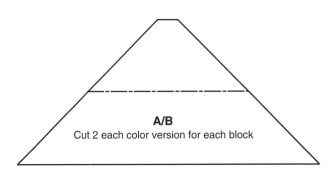

A/B
Cut 2 each color version for each block

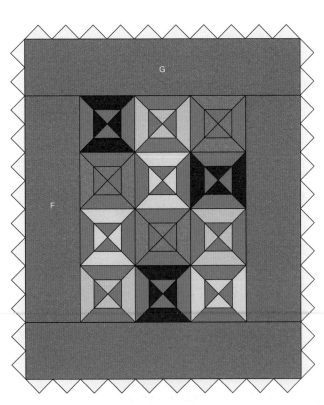

Spools Variation
Placement Diagram 10" x 12"
(without prairie points)

Churn Dash Delight

Red and green combine with a light background to make a mini that is a perfect holiday accent piece.

Project Specifications
Skill Level: Advanced
Quilt Size: 12" x 14½"
Block Size: 2½" x 2½"
Number of Blocks: 6

Project Notes
The Churn Dash block has always been a big hit with quilters. It can be set on point in a different quilt plan. Choose a good color contrast for the small-size blocks.

Materials
- 1 fat quarter beige solid
- 1 fat quarter red print
- 6" x 10" rectangle green print
- ⅛ yard green-with-gold print
- ⅛ yard beige plaid
- 14" x 16½" lightweight batting
- 15" x 17½" backing
- Neutral-color all-purpose thread
- Cream and red quilting thread
- Basic sewing tools and supplies, 3" x 18" ruler and 4" Baby Bias Square ruler

Cutting
Note: Use the 3" x 18" ruler to cut 45-degree bias strips; reverse cutting direction if left-handed.

1. Cut an 11" x 18" rectangle beige solid; subcut into four 1½" x 15" bias strips for A referring to Figure 1. From remaining fabric, cut four 1" x 8" strips for B.

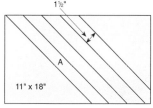

Figure 1   **Figure 2**

2. Cut an 11" x 18" rectangle red print; lay the red print rectangle wrong side up on a flat surface; cut four 1½" x 15" bias strips for C as shown in Figure 2. Cut one 1" x 8" strip from remaining fabric for D and four 2½" x 2½" squares for I.

Churn Dash
2½" x 2½" Block
Make 6

3. Cut four 1" x 8" strips green print for E.

4. Cut six 3" x 3" squares beige plaid for F.

5. Cut two strips each 2½" x 10½" G and 2½" x 8" H green-with-gold print.

6. Cut 1"-wide strips red print and join to create a 62" binding strip referring to Binding Your Quilt on page 20.

Piecing Blocks
Note: Use 4" Baby Bias Square ruler to cut bias squares or prepare A/C template using pattern given. Use a ¼" seam allowance; press seams before trimming. Press all seams in the direction of small arrows shown on figure drawings.

1. Join A and C bias strips with right sides together along length; repeat for four strip sets. Cut (24) 1½" x 1½" A/C bias squares using bias ruler or template A/C, matching line on template to seam between strips as shown in Figure 3.

Figure 3

2. Join one B and E strip with right sides together along length; repeat for two strip sets. Trim seams to ⅛", press and cut into (12) 1"-wide B/E segments as shown in Figure 4.

Figure 4

3. Join two A/C units with one B/E segment as shown in Figure 5; repeat for 12 units.

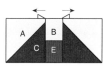

Figure 5

4. Join 1" x 8" strips with right sides together to make a B/E/D/E/B strip set; trim seams to 1/8" and press. Cut six 1" segments from the strip.

5. Sew a B/E/D/E/B segment between two A/C/B/E units, matching seams as shown in Figure 6 to complete one block; repeat for six blocks.

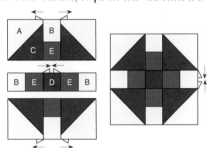

Figure 6

Piecing the Top

1. Join two blocks with F to make a row as shown in Figure 7; repeat for two rows and press.

2. Join two F squares with one block to make a row, again referring to Figure 7; repeat for two rows and press.

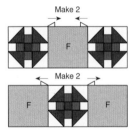

Figure 7

3. Join the rows referring to the Placement Diagram for positioning; press seams in one direction.

4. Sew a G strip to opposite long sides of the pieced center; press. Sew I to each end of each H strip; press.

5. Sew an H/I strip to the top and bottom of the pieced center to complete the top.

Finishing

1. Press quilt top on both sides; check for proper seam pressing and trim all loose threads.

2. Mark top for quilting. *Note: The quilt shown was hand-quilted in a diagonal grid through the centers and from seam points on blocks to border strips as shown in Figure 8, in an X on I squares and in the ditch of seams using cream quilting thread. Red quilting thread was used to hand-quilt two centered lines 1/2" apart on each G and H border strips.*

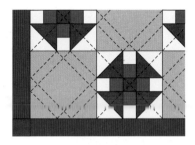

Figure 8

3. Sandwich batting between the stitched top and the backing piece; pin or baste layers together to hold. Quilt as desired by hand or machine.

4. When quilting is complete, trim batting and backing fabric even with raw edges of quilt top.

5. Bind edges with 1"-wide red print prepared binding strips referring to Binding Your Quilt on page 20. ❖

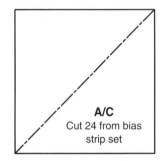

A/C
Cut 24 from bias strip set

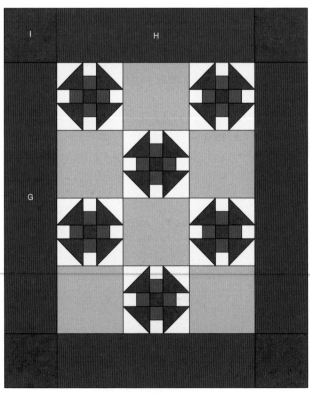

Churn Dash Delight
Placement Diagram 12" x 14½"

Homecoming

Take a weekend off and stitch up a quilt of house blocks in any color combination.

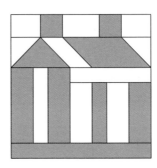

House
4¾" x 4¾" Block
Make 4

Project Specifications
Skill Level: Easy
Quilt Size: 16½" x 16½"
Block Size: 4¾" x 4¾"
Number of Blocks: 4

Materials
- 9" x 18" rectangle each four assorted prints for house prints
- 5" x 9" rectangle blue solid
- ½ fat quarter blue floral
- Fat quarter white solid
- ⅛ yard blue print for binding
- Backing 19½" x 19½"
- Batting 18½" x 18½"
- Neutral-color all-purpose thread
- White quilting thread
- Basic sewing tools and supplies and Quilter's Rule™ Mini Triangle 45-degree ruler

Cutting
1. Cut the following from white solid: eight 1¼" x 1½" A rectangles; four 1¼" x 1¾" B rectangles; four 1⅞" x 1⅞" squares for C; four 1" x 3⅛" D strips; four 1" x 3" E strips; four 1" x 3¼" F strips; eight 1¼" x 2½" G strips; and (12) 1½" x 5¼" H strips.

2. Cut the following from each of the house prints: two 1¼" x 1¼" I squares; one 2¼" x 2¼" J square; one 1½" x 4¼" K strip; two 1¼" x 3" L strips; one 1" x 2½" M strip; one 1¼" x 2½" N strip; and one 1" x 5¼" O strip.

3. Cut nine 1½" x 1½" P squares blue solid.

4. Cut two 2¼" x 13" Q strips and two 2¼" x 16½" R strips blue floral.

5. Cut 1"-wide strips blue print and join to create a 74" binding strip referring to Binding Your Quilt on page 20.

Piecing Blocks
Note: Use a ¼" seam allowance; press seams before trimming. Press all seams in the direction of small arrows shown on figure drawings. Use the same house print pieces to complete one house block.

1. To piece one block, join two A rectangles, two matching I squares and one B rectangle to make a 5¼" chimney unit as shown in Figure 1.

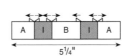

Figure 1 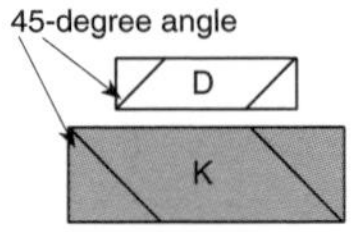   **Figure 2**

2. With right sides up and using the mini triangle tool, cut 45-degree triangles off each end of the D pieces to make a parallelogram as shown in Figure 2. Repeat with K strips, again referring to Figure 2.

3. Cut each C square in half on one diagonal to make C triangles; repeat with J to make J triangles.

4. Join matching J and K pieces with D and two C triangles as shown in Figure 3 to make a roof unit.

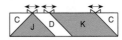

Figure 3

5. Join two matching L strips with E to make a door unit as shown in Figure 4.

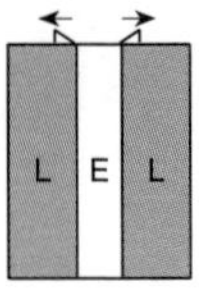

Figure 4

6. Join two G strips with matching M and N strips, and add F to make a window unit as shown in Figure 5.

Figure 5

7. Join a matching door and window unit to make a house unit as shown in Figure 6.

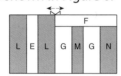

Figure 6

8. Join the chimney, roof and house units as shown in Figure 7.

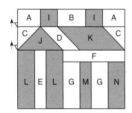

Figure 7

9. Sew O to the bottom of the pieced unit to complete one House block as shown in Figure 8; repeat for four House blocks.

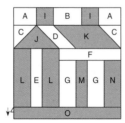

Figure 8

Piecing the Top

1. Join two House blocks with three H strips to make a block row as shown in Figure 9; repeat for two block rows. Press seams toward H.

Figure 9

2. Join two H strips and three P squares to make a sashing row as shown in Figure 10; repeat for three sashing rows. Press seams toward H.

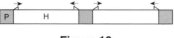

Figure 10

3. Join the block rows with the sashing rows to complete the pieced center; press seams toward sashing rows.

4. Sew Q to opposite sides and R to the top and bottom of the pieced center; press seams toward Q and R to complete the pieced top.

Finishing

1. Press quilt top on both sides; check for proper seam pressing and trim all loose threads.

2. Mark top for quilting if using patterned design. *Note: The quilt shown was hand-quilted in the ditch of seams and with an X through the center of each P square using cream hand-quilting thread.*

3. Sandwich batting between the stitched top and the backing piece; pin or baste layers together to hold. Quilt as desired by hand or machine.

4. When quilting is complete, trim batting and backing fabric even with raw edges of quilt top.

5. Bind edges with 1"-wide blue print prepared binding strips referring to Binding Your Quilt on page 20. ❖

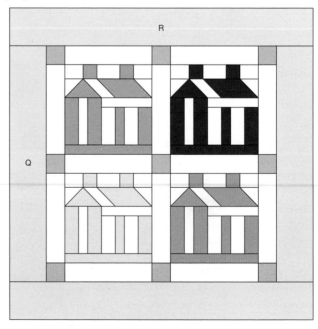

Homecoming
Placement Diagram 16½" x 16½"

Dainty Baskets

Tiny basket blocks float on a light-color background in this pretty basket quilt.

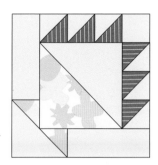

Dainty Basket
2½" x 2½" Block
Make 5

Project Specifications
Skill Level: Intermediate
Quilt Size: 11" x 11"
Block Size: 2½" x 2½"
Number of Blocks: 5

Materials
- 1 fat quarter tan mottled for background
- 1 fat quarter blue stripe
- 1 fat quarter floral print
- 13" x 13" lightweight batting
- 14" x 14" backing
- Neutral-color all-purpose thread
- Cream quilting thread
- Basic sewing tools and supplies, 3" x 18" ruler and 4" Baby Bias Square ruler

Cutting
Note: Use the 3" x 18" ruler to cut 45-degree bias strips; reverse cutting direction if left-handed.

1. Cut one 11" x 18" rectangle tan mottled; place wrong side up on a flat surface. Cut four 1" x 15" A bias strips as shown in Figure 1.

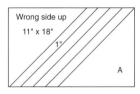

Wrong side up
11" x 18"
1"
A

Figure 1

2. From the remaining tan mottled, cut five 1" x 1" B squares, three 2⅜" x 2⅜" C squares, ten 1" x 2" D pieces, three 1⅞" x 1⅞" E squares, one 4¾" x 4¾" I square and two 2⅝" x 2⅝" J squares.

3. Cut two 11" x 16" rectangles blue stripe; place pieces right side up on a flat surface; referring to Figure 2, cut two 1" x 15" F bias strips from each piece, reversing direction of strips on each piece.

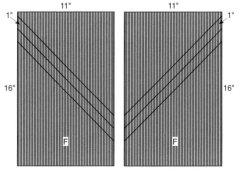

11" 1"   11" 1"
16"   16"
F   F

Figure 2

4. From the floral print cut three 2⅜" x 2⅜" G squares, five 1⅜" x 1⅜" H squares and four 2¼" x 13" K strips.

5. Cut 1"-wide strips floral print and join to create a 52" binding strip referring to Binding Your Quilt on page 20.

Piecing Blocks
Note: Use 4" Baby Bias Square ruler to cut bias squares or prepare A/F template using pattern given. Use a ¼" seam allowance; press seams before trimming. Press all seams in the direction of small arrows shown on figure drawings.

1. Sew one A bias strip to one F bias strip to make an A/F strip set; repeat for four strip sets.

2. Cut 30 A/F 1" x 1" bias squares from strip set with 15 squares with stripes running in one direction and 15 squares with stripes running in the opposite direction as shown in Figure 3.

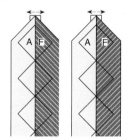

A F   A F

Figure 3

3. Cut C and G squares in half on one diagonal to make six each C and G triangles. Discard one triangle of each fabric.

4. Sew C to G to make a C/G unit as shown in Figure 4; repeat for five units. Press seams open and trim corner tails referring to Figure 5.

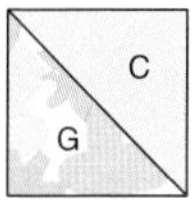

C   C
G   G

Figure 4 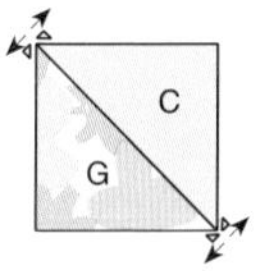   **Figure 5**

House of White Birches, Berne, Indiana 46711 Clotilde.com

5. Join three matching A/F bias squares to make a set as shown in Figure 6; repeat for 10 sets, again referring to Figure 6.

6. Sew one A/F set to one C/G square to make an A/F/C/G unit as shown in Figure 7; repeat for five units.

7. Join one A/F set and one B square to make an A/F/B unit as shown in Figure 8; repeat for five units.

Make 5

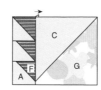

Make 5

Figure 6

Figure 7

Figure 8

8. Sew one A/F/B unit to one A/F/C/G unit, matching seams as shown in Figure 9; repeat for five units.

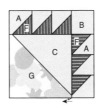

Figure 9

9. Cut H squares in half on one diagonal to make 10 H triangles.

10. Sew one D strip to one H triangle to make a set as shown in Figure 10; repeat for five sets and five sets reversed.

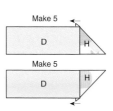

Figure 10

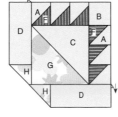

Figure 11

11. Sew a D/H and D/H reversed unit to the previously pieced units as shown in Figure 11.

12. Cut E squares in half on one diagonal to make six E triangles; discard one triangle.

13. Sew an E triangle to each previously pieced unit to complete five Dainty Basket blocks referring to Figure 12.

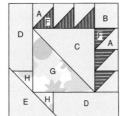

Figure 12

Dainty Baskets
Placement Diagram 11" x 11"

Piecing the Top

1. Cut the I square in half on both diagonals to make four I triangles.

2. Arrange blocks and I triangles in three diagonal rows as shown in Figure 13; join in rows.

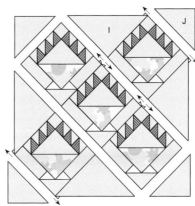

Figure 13

3. Cut J squares in half on one diagonal to make four J triangles. Sew a J triangle to each corner of the pieced section to complete the pieced center, again referring to Figure 13.

4. Sew a K strip to each side of the pieced center and miter corners referring to Borders on page 13; trim excess. Press seams toward K.

Finishing

1. Press quilt top on both sides; check for proper seam pressing and trim all loose threads.

2. Sandwich batting between the stitched top and the backing piece; pin or baste layers together to hold. Quilt as desired by hand or machine. *Note: The quilt shown was hand-quilted in the ditch of seams, ¼" from seams in C/G units and in the heart quilting design given with Kaleidoscope on page 34 on the border strips using cream quilting thread.*

3. When quilting is complete, trim batting and backing fabric even with raw edges of quilt top.

4. Bind edges with 1"-wide floral print prepared binding strips referring to Binding Your Quilt on page 20. ❖

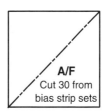

A/F
Cut 30 from bias strip sets

Charming Log Cabin

Instructions on page 36

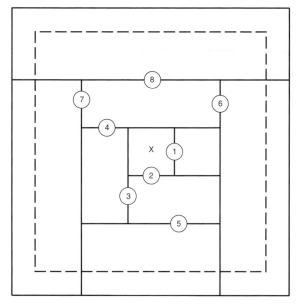

Unit A Paper-Piecing Pattern
Make 12 copies

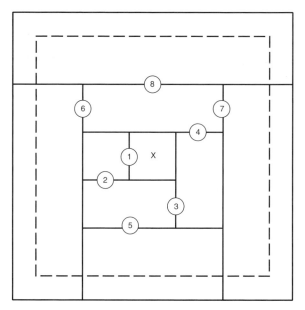

Unit B Paper-Piecing Pattern
Make 12 copies

Meet the Designer

An avid crafter, Christine Carlson never dreamt that one day, purely by chance, she would become a professional miniature quiltmaker, author, designer, teacher and lecturer.

Having only a few fabrics on hand, no quiltmaking skills to speak of, and no rotary tools or sewing machine, she made her first miniature quilt as a personal challenge; she would be the first to admit that it was not very attractive or well made. To encourage students new to miniature quiltmaking, Christine proudly uses this quilt as an example that no matter the outcome, everyone has to start somewhere.

Again, purely by chance, Christine got a job managing a small quilt shop, and it was there she learned important quiltmaking skills. She developed these skills while creating wall quilts, large-size quilts and various quilt projects for teaching classes using rotary tools and a sewing machine.

These skills led her to a love of miniature quiltmaking and being hooked forever to minis. She now has over 200 miniature quilts to her credit. With patience and perseverance, she has graduated to publishing this, her third book, as well as many quilt magazine patterns and articles on miniature quiltmaking.

In time, all this quilt interest led to a new love, that of collecting and studying about vintage fabrics from different eras. To make historically correct miniature quilts, Christine uses only era-related fabric in any one quilt. However, Christine also delights in using many of the new quilt fabrics that are just perfect for her first love of miniature quiltmaking.

Metric Conversion Charts

Metric Conversions

Canada/U.S. Measurement			Multiplied by		Metric Measurement
yards	x	.9144	=		metres (m)
yards	x	91.44	=		centimetres (cm)
inches	x	2.54	=		centimetres (cm)
inches	x	25.40	=		millimetres (mm)
inches	x	.0254	=		metres (m)

Canada/U.S. Measurement			Multiplied by		Metric Measurement
centimetres	x	.3937	=		inches
metres	x	1.0936	=		yards

Standard Equivalents

Canada/U.S. Measurement		Metric Measurement			Canada/U.S. Measurement		Metric Measurement		
⅛ inch	=	3.20 mm	=	0.32 cm	1⅜ yards	=	125.73 cm	=	1.26 m
¼ inch	=	6.35 mm	=	0.635 cm	1½ yards	=	137.16 cm	=	1.37 m
⅜ inch	=	9.50 mm	=	0.95 cm	1⅝ yards	=	148.59 cm	=	1.49 m
½ inch	=	12.70 mm	=	1.27 cm	1¾ yards	=	160.02 cm	=	1.60 m
⅝ inch	=	15.90 mm	=	1.59 cm	1⅞ yards	=	171.44 cm	=	1.71 m
¾ inch	=	19.10 mm	=	1.91 cm	2 yards	=	182.88 cm	=	1.83 m
⅞ inch	=	22.20 mm	=	2.22 cm	2⅛ yards	=	194.31 cm	=	1.94 m
1 inch	=	25.40 mm	=	2.54 cm	2¼ yards	=	205.74 cm	=	2.06 m
⅛ yard	=	11.43 cm	=	0.11 m	2⅜ yards	=	217.17 cm	=	2.17 m
¼ yard	=	22.86 cm	=	0.23 m	2½ yards	=	228.60 cm	=	2.29 m
⅜ yard	=	34.29 cm	=	0.34 m	2⅝ yards	=	240.03 cm	=	2.40 m
½ yard	=	45.72 cm	=	0.46 m	2¾ yards	=	251.46 cm	=	2.51 m
⅝ yard	=	57.15 cm	=	0.57 m	2⅞ yards	=	262.88 cm	=	2.63 m
¾ yard	=	68.58 cm	=	0.69 m	3 yards	=	274.32 cm	=	2.74 m
⅞ yard	=	80.00 cm	=	0.80 m	3⅛ yards	=	285.75 cm	=	2.86 m
1 yard	=	91.44 cm	=	0.91 m	3¼ yards	=	297.18 cm	=	2.97 m
1⅛ yards	=	102.87 cm	=	1.03 m	3⅜ yards	=	308.61 cm	=	3.09 m
1¼ yards	=	114.30 cm	=	1.14 m	3½ yards	=	320.04 cm	=	3.20 m
					3⅝ yards	=	331.47 cm	=	3.31 m
					3¾ yards	=	342.90 cm	=	3.43 m
					3⅞ yards	=	354.32 cm	=	3.54 m
					4 yards	=	365.76 cm	=	3.66 m
					4⅛ yards	=	377.19 cm	=	3.77 m
					4¼ yards	=	388.62 cm	=	3.89 m
					4⅜ yards	=	400.05 cm	=	4.00 m
					4½ yards	=	411.48 cm	=	4.11 m
					4⅝ yards	=	422.91 cm	=	4.23 m
					4¾ yards	=	434.34 cm	=	4.34 m
					4⅞ yards	=	445.76 cm	=	4.46 m
					5 yards	=	457.20 cm	=	4.57 m

Make Mine Mini is published by DRG, 306 East Parr Road, Berne, IN 46711. Printed in USA. Copyright © 2010 DRG. All rights reserved. This publication may not be reproduced in part or in whole without written permission from the publisher.

RETAIL STORES: If you would like to carry this pattern book or any other DRG publications, visit DRGwholesale.com

Every effort has been made to ensure that the instructions in this pattern book are complete and accurate. We cannot, however, take responsibility for human error, typographical mistakes or variations in individual work. Please visit ClotildeCustomerCare.com to check for pattern updates.

HOUSE of WHITE BIRCHES
PUBLISHERS SINCE 1947

ISBN: 978-1-59217-323-5
1 2 3 4 5 6 7 8 9

Photo Index